The Great Questions of Life

There's only ever been one idea in art.
You know, the Gauguin questions:
  Where do we come from?
  What are we?
  Where are we going?[1]
  What's it all about, Alfie?

Damien Hirst, quoted in an interview
by Martin Gayford, *Daily Telegraph*,
February 28, 2004

Don Cupitt

Library of Congress Cataloging-in-Publication Data

Cupitt, Don.
    The great questions of life / Don Cupitt.
        p. cm.
    Includes bibliographical references (p.) and index.
    ISBN 0-944344-56-9
    1. Life. 2. Life--Religious aspects--Christianity. 3. Religion--Philosophy. 4. Knowledge, Theory of (Religion) 5. Meaning (Philosophy)--Religious aspects--Christianity. I. Title.

BD431.C95 2005
210--dc22

                                                              2004063523

1 *D'ou Venons Nous*
Que Sommes Nous
Ou Allons-Nous

Inscription by Gauguin on the top left-
hand corner of his big painting of 1897,
in the Museum of Fine Arts, Boston

Contents

Introduction

In a rather piecemeal fashion, I have been trying since about 1999 to work out the theology of a new kind of religion. It is a popular and post-institutional faith that may perhaps be seen as deriving from the tradition of Hegel and existentialism. In Hegel's day people were coming to see the end of *L'Ancien Régime* as marking the end of the old hierarchical conception of reality, and its replacement by a new story that sees everything as developing historically within an entirely immanent process. In Hegel's interpretation of modernity, with the end of classical metaphysics the entire supernatural world of religion has come down from heaven and been dispersed into the unfolding common life of humanity. Ecclesiastical Christianity as we have known it hitherto reaches fulfilment and comes to an end. Instead of being routed through the heavenly world above, religion becomes immediate and beliefless, and the love of God is transposed into a new and ardent love of and commitment to life.

Since Hegel and the existentialists, this little cluster of ideas has been clarified and elaborated in various ways, and has become the stock-in-trade of radical theology. The change in religion that it implies may be compared with the change in politics from absolute monarchy to liberal democracy, in ecclesiology from 'the church' to 'the kingdom', and in morals from conscience and the moral law to the lifestyle ethics of today.

So far, so (apparently) straightforward; but many sceptical readers will surely be wondering what the 'theology' of a beliefless and immediately lived type of religion can possibly look like. I began to study the philoso-

1

phy of religion in the academical year 1954–55, during the course of which the then Knightbridge Professor of Moral Philosophy at Cambridge, R.B. Braithwaite, put forward one of the first and most intensively discussed noncognitive theories of religion, and I well remember the incredulity—indeed, the hilarity—that greeted his views.[1] Braithwaite had recently been converted, and was a sincere believer who yet didn't think that any standard beliefs were actually 'true', in the usual philistine British sense. For Braithwaite, to say the Creed was simply to declare your allegiance to the Christian way of life, as illustrated in various doctrinal stories, parables, and so forth. That made him a non-realist[2] *avant la lettre*—a bewildering position to people in 1955. How *could* there be religion without beliefs? Seeking baptism, Braithwaite had endeavoured to explain his views to the then Bishop of Ely, Noel Hudson, who was a kindly man but notoriously a Bear of Very Little Brain (as bishops so often are), and there were many attempts to reconstruct their conversation.

All this is comical in retrospect, but it reminds us that both in 1955 and in 2006 nearly everybody's view of religion remains intensely dogmatic-Platonist. Knowledge matters most of all. Objective Truth matters most of all. The job of religion is to give us—and to help us to believe—some very reassuring information about how things really are for us behind the scenes—information about God, God's love for us, God's forgiveness of our sins, and God's offer of eternal bliss in the heavenly world after death. The news sounds almost too good to be true, but God will give us faith. Anyway, we are talking about information and about Objective Truth. That's what matters most, and that is why to this day people think that the essence of religion must consist of a group of dogmatic beliefs—beliefs that convey news about how things are for us in a more real world beyond the apparent world. For most people, religious persons just are believers. Such people cannot imagine how religion could be really interesting and demanding without centering around doctrinal beliefs. Supernatural doctrines, understood in a realist sense, are what American idiom calls 'the beef'. So when I say that I don't believe that there *is* any further reality beyond the human world, and declare for thoroughgoing 'linguistic naturalism' or 'Empty radical humanism', people mentally switch off. They assume that without the primacy of knowledge, and in particular of supernatural belief, there can be no religion.

It is not easy to change that assumption. As William James used to say, people seem to have got themselves into the way of supposing that the menu is a much greater thing than the food, and that supernatural beliefs *about* religion, held by faith and upon authority, are bigger and more interesting than the actual lived life *of* religion to which those beliefs are meant to lead us. But there it is: people's ideas about religion have gradually come to be all the wrong way round, and we have to chip away very slowly as we try to undo all the misconceptions.

A number of new ideas will need to be proposed. Thus in the present book I mention a distinction between 'Microsoft theology' and 'Linux theology'. In Microsoft theology the operating system—the set of beliefs and practices—that you live by and work with is 'proprietary': that is, it is tied to a particular institution and its power structure. Somebody owns the rights, and demands his or her cut from you. But the newer Linux theology is 'open source': that is, even the 'highest' religious truth is thought of as being out in public and freely available to all. Nobody has been granted the franchise for it. You can use it, tweak it, add to it, just as you please. It is not sacrosanct: it is completely democratized.

The kind of theology to which we have been accustomed is proprietary, Microsoft theology. There has always been a close link between religious truth and claims about institutional rights and power. I'm trying to introduce a Linux theology breaks that link. It is post-institutional, and in many ways represents a return to the days in antiquity when religious thought and philosophical thinking more or less coincided.

I sometimes call my new way of working 'democratic philosophy'. Instead of constantly referring to and quoting from a small canon of Great Men who are regarded as authorities, I try hard to keep close to the idioms of ordinary language and the way the language is currently developing—my working assumption being that the thought of ordinary people will turn out to be interesting and important. The newest popular phrases are often surprisingly sophisticated, and the changes in religious thought that they embody are going on simultaneously all around the world. Thus, a few weeks before writing these words I was talking to a Danish audience about the new English life-idioms. I quoted the vivid and brutal new phrase from the late 1980s, **Get a life!** as our modern equivalent for the old religious demand that one must begin a new and converted life, but I soon discovered that there was no need to labour the point. 'Oh', said someone, 'we've already taken that English phrase, without translating it, straight into colloquial Danish.'

More astonishingly, my translators assured me that the points I'd been trying to make about the way ordinary language is currently moving are equally familiar in China! The truth seems to be that apart from a few ultraconservative pockets within Islam, the whole of humanity nowadays takes part in a single global conversation, within which a major religious shift is taking place. Roughly, we are changing over from a very long-termist, otherworldly, and mediated religion of eternal salvation in another world beyond death to a very short-termist, this-worldly, and immediate religion of ethical commitment to this life, here and now. This new form of religiosity is not only democratic; one may call it ultra-urban. (To explain this last word, I should say that ever since the late Middle Ages in Europe it has been noticed that urban religious life is more volatile, emotional, and short-termist than rural religion.)

Many of us still hesitate: you will see in the discussion of the Great Questions of Life how many of them are framed in a way that betrays intense, aching nostalgia for the old worldview that has recently collapsed. And I know what you'll tell me: you'll be able to change over *decisively* to the new religion and worldview only when you are really persuaded that it is going to be a great improvement on what we have lost. So far, you are not fully persuaded, and you keep one foot in each camp. But we must overcome that debilitating nostalgia. It's killing us.

One way to persuade people that they really must commit themselves *now* to the only life they'll ever have is by introducing and explaining the idea that this world, the human lifeworld, the only world, is *outsideless*. I think people are fairly well accustomed by now to the idea that the universe of modern physics is finite but unbounded, i.e., outsideless. There is no way out of it: you never bump into any wall around it. Rather similarly, every word in an ordinary English dictionary is explained in terms of other words which are also to be found in the dictionary, and so on, forever. A living vernacular language is a complete world with no outside. You never reach any last word that points out of language, and attaches the whole network of language to something 'real' outside it, as a hammock is attached to a tree, because the world of linguistic meaning is also finite but unbounded. A dictionary, and indeed every printed book, contains only signs that are connected with other signs, words that lead on sideways to other words. There's no way that a printer could find a way of including in a printed dictionary a word that points off the page, out of language altogether, and into extralinguistic 'reality'. What printed mark could ever do that job? A linguistic sign can 'mean' only other signs. Anyway, what could a supposed extralinguistic reality be? Can you find some medium *other than* language in which you can tell me all about it? Of course you cannot, for as the old, hard saying has it: 'Language is only about itself'. Our language has already incorporated our whole world within itself: do we understand that?

So the universe of physics is outsideless, and the world of language is outsideless: similarly, and still more important, the language-formed human lifeworld is outsidelessly all there is. The world that our talk is all the time making and modifying is the only world: it's all there is. All attempts to get out of it only come circling back into it.

Once you begin to grasp the implications of outsidelessness, you will get the shivers. It is a strange, terrifying, numinous non-idea. Meditating upon it *accurately* is going to be important in the growth and development of the new religious outlook. But more of that anon. For now, I need to issue a warning: don't assume that outsidelessness is God, or a fancy postmodern substitute for God. The situation is a bit stranger than that.

* * * * *

Although we often hear people talk about the 'big', or the 'ultimate', or the 'great' questions, it soon becomes apparent in this book that our language does not have agreed standard ways of specifying just what they are, except that they are about what the comic Science Fiction writer Douglas Adams called *Life, the Universe and Everything*. In addition, most people seem not to have thought about what sort of *answers* they are looking for. They may ask, *What are we here for? What's it all about?* or *What is the meaning of life?* but they rarely pause to think about what method of enquiry might be appropriate if one really wants to have rational answers to such questions.

Because of this vagueness, I cannot here use the 'democratic', ordinary-language method quite so systematically as in the earlier life-books of 1999 and 2003. Instead of quoting stock phrases in bold type, I simply use italics for phrases and short sentences that are (as I hope you'll agree) typical of what one frequently hears in everyday speech. The bold-type phrases are nowadays being listed in dictionaries, whereas sentences such as *What is the purpose of life?* and *Where have all the flowers gone?* and their many variants are not. Nevertheless, I *am* here persisting with and even taking further my highly heretical idea that the seemingly rather-woolly ideas of ordinary people about 'the meaning of life' are of philosophical interest, and that the so-called Great Questions of Life deserve to be collected and given a closer examination than they have ever previously received.

Commenting on my recent work, some friends have suggested that I am trying to reduce both philosophy of life and theology to sociology. Not quite: as I see it, I am taking up and pushing a bit further some of Wittgenstein's ideas. We need to pay more attention to the worldview and the religion that comes with ordinariness, because ordinariness is the furthest back we can get, and from it everything else is built out. It is with us, and it constrains us, rather more than we might suppose. It's *wily*, it's unexpectedly quick on the uptake, and it deserves more respect than it is usually accorded.

Some of these ideas have been presented at meetings and conferences here and there. Chapter 1 was delivered as an address at the Westar Institute's Spring Meeting in New York City in March 2004.

Cambridge, 2004
D.C.

BEGINNING ALL OVER AGAIN

On May 8, 1942, as the United States entered the Second World War, Vice President Henry Wallace declared in a much-quoted speech that

> The century on which we are entering—the century which will come out of this war—can be and must be the century of the common man.[1]

Sixty years later, there is general agreement among us about who, in the century of the common man, has become the common man of the century. He is Homer Simpson. By now Matt Groening and his team are said to have issued over 360 episodes of *The Simpsons*—an astounding figure—and Homer's world has been described in great detail. He is the modern Everyman, especially of the advanced countries, especially of the liberal Protestant English-speaking world, and most especially of Middle America.

It is often said that Americans are not good at irony, but the pleasure *The Simpsons* gives us is precisely the pleasure of irony. By deft scriptwriting all points of view and all aspects of the Simpsons' world are mercilessly mocked, but it is done with such unfailing good humour and lightness of touch that we end up, like his gifted daughter Lisa, by loving Homer just as he is and with all his manifest absurdities. In fact the films themselves carry an important religious message, for they first help us to transcend small-town ordinariness, see its limits, and laugh at it, and second they *also* help us to return into ordinariness and accept it because in the end it is all there is. Matt Groening is the Jane Austen of our late Modern age, for both Groening and Austen faced the same question: How is a thinking person to cope with the banality and narrowness of ordinary life? Answer: By using her intelligence to see it as it is, to see through it, rise above it, and laugh at it—and learn to do all this with such generosity of spirit that she is enabled to return into ordinariness and accept it, because it is out-sideless, and because it is all we'll ever know. There is no more real world beyond: there is no place elsewhere that will compensate us for the banal-ity of Springfield. Springfield is all there is, and the joyful wisdom is to say a good humoured and wholehearted yes to it, just as it is.

From what I have said you will gather that I agree with all those who say that *The Simpsons* is a considerable work of art, a divine comedy whose message is substantially correct. But it doesn't follow that everything *with-in* the world of Springfield is perfect. Far from it: and in particular I must draw your attention to the state of religion in that town. Many religions and para-religious movements are mentioned, but only two are perma-nent social facts and live options[2] for most of the characters. There is the Evangelical Protestantism of Ned Flanders and his family, which even Homer can see is goofy and immature and on which we need not spend much time here, and there is the 'mainline' or liberal Protestantism of the middle-of-the-road church that the Simpsons themselves attend. It may be Episcopalian, it may be Methodist, it may be Presbyterian. No matter: the most interesting figure at the church is the minister, who is known (again ironically) as 'Reverend Lovejoy'. He is a melancholy and rather tragic character who clearly knows in his heart that the religion to which he has given his life has become an intellectual and spiritual disaster. When he was in training thirty years ago, his teachers assured him, and he believed, that 'a critical orthodoxy' was possible. Christianity and modernity were compatible. But the attrition of the years has worn his faith down, and he well knows how hollow the old answers sound today. Unfortunately they are all he's got, and he has to go on parroting them.

The scriptwriters are cruel about Lovejoy's dilemma here. For example, when he is confronted by people's bewilderment in the face of tragedy, he knows he has to affirm the objective reality both of God's power and of God's love, so the best consolation he can offer is the uplifting thought that 'God loves his victims'.

Still more devastating is the portrayal of the Simpson family at church. Look at their faces: Homer and Bart are bored rigid. They are here only because Marge makes them come. Marge herself radiates her characteristic vague benignity: she approves of church and thinks it's where the family ought to be on a Sunday, but the truth is that she has no more idea of what's going on there than Maggie has. Only Lisa looks really alert: she's busily working out what it all means. Everything interests Lisa. There will always be one or two Lisas around, but the extent to which they can help normal people is strictly limited.

Many observers of the American religious scene think it a remarkable fact that Americans remain seemingly so much more religious than the people of any other advanced country. Where else in the world do the Homer Simpsons still attend church? Where else can we imagine them one day returning to churchgoing? Nowhere: but is this a good reason for being optimistic and talking about American exceptionalism? *The Simpsons* suggests not, for it portrays a world in which the old religion is no longer understood, is no longer imaginatively inspiring, and no longer makes any appreciable and important difference to people's lives. People do know that religion matters, and matters a lot; but their own religion is already in terminal decline. They are still turning up dutifully, but it makes no sense and is doing them no good. They're bored. It is true that Ned Flanders' religion still makes a perceptible difference to his life; but who wants to be like Ned Flanders? Summing up his own version of the Christian life, Ned says: 'You name it, I haven't done it'—which says it all.

Why has this catastrophe happened? The shortest and simplest answer is that the old premodern and 'tradition-directed' type of human being was trained by culture to see everything and to build his world in terms of a great block of grand normative ideas—'absolutes', myths, religious doctrines and images. That is how religion used to work. Almost nothing was seen as it was: everything was seen and estimated in its relation to the ideal order. Not surprisingly, everything was seen not as itself, but in terms of how far it fell short of the divine perfection. Everyone was a sinner, and everything fell short. They had almost no knowledge in those days, but they did have an absolute standard against which they measured everything, and so they could claim to 'know the difference between right and wrong'. But we post-Enlightenment modern people are very different. We have huge amounts of empirical knowledge, but no 'absolute' truth. We have set aside all the old normative ideas, and instead have covered the world all over with our own minutely detailed empirical descriptions and theories. This new way of building our world has turned out to be hugely powerful, and the results are in many ways beautiful—but it has left the older ways of thinking, religious, moral, and philosophical, stranded and unable to function properly. It has also given us a very different world.

A simple example of the changeover is given by the current controversies about 'gay bishops' and the like. Until the Enlightenment most people could characterize others and fix some knowledge about them only by passing moral judgment upon them. There was no scientific psychology: there was only moral judgment, which enabled you to classify another person as a miser, or a glutton, or a coward, or whatever. People resembled Snow White's seven dwarves, each of whom has only one identifying characteristic. So people were seen as embodying universal qualities—virtues or vices. Everybody was an emblem of the vice or the virtue that she typified. But then at about the time of the Romantic Movement modern psychology began. We began gradually to develop many new ways of describing other people and explaining how they develop and how they tick—and all this new vocabulary soon made the old simpleminded moralism redundant. For the first time in the history of Western thought it became possible to see homosexuality as involving more than just a class of actions that were known in advance to be morally wrong: people could now learn to look at homosexuality empirically and see it as a certain constitution of the whole personality, and as a way that some people happen to have developed. There's room here for debate about how it happens that different people come to develop different sexualities or sexual orientations, but there's no room for the old reflex moral condemnation. It is uninformative: it doesn't really *tell* us anything. Consider, for example, the way we are sometimes pressed to agree that someone or other is 'evil'. We feel reluctant and embarrassed. Sorry, no: that word darkens counsel. Its use creates a feeling of righteous satisfaction, but sheds no light at all.

In many of the advanced countries the two ways of thinking are nevertheless still struggling against each other. Many ordinary people cling to the old moralism and the old black-and-white view of the world, while in the universities and in 'the caring professions' others try to persuade them that it's better to work in the modern way, by building up agreed descriptions, explanatory theories, and ways of understanding and coping. The conflict is fierce, and one popular (not to say, *populist*) way of managing it is to keep the new ways of thinking securely locked up in the universities, where they can't get out and cause any more harm in what is called 'the real world'. In Britain, people tend to see it like that, because we are terrified of the new ways of thinking. Above all, we are terrified that if they are applied to religion and morality they will destroy everything we hold dear. So we insist that the universities must not actively spread new ideas, but must instead *act as prisons* for new ideas. At the same time, we hide from ourselves the truth of what we are doing by ridiculing university people as idle dreamers who live in ivory towers! By this ingenious double manoeuvre, the British try to insulate themselves from new ideas and keep their traditional religious vocabulary intact.

To return to Homer Simpson and his family, sitting in a row in their church, I think we now understand better what the cartoons are saying. Like many other people the world over, Springfield folk continue to cling obdurately to their ancestral faith, even though it now does not work and makes no sense at all, having in fact died some generations ago. But the present rather strained, awkward period cannot continue for much longer, and it's obvious enough that people like Homer and Bart will not still be sitting in their places a few years from now. In English Roman Catholicism I remember the way the last Irish Homer Simpsons used to sit farther and farther back during Sunday Mass. Then for a time they could be seen *standing* at the back, hanging about awkwardly, until in the end they disappeared altogether. And the basic philosophical event that underlies this withdrawal is that we have collectively changed over from one way of world-building to another. We used to see everything and to build our world in terms of great normative moral and religious ideas. They were all we had to build our world with, and they seemed to be enough. In the Muslim heartlands there are still a few people who construct their world in that way, people for whom religion alone is the source of all knowledge. Everything is seen and judged in relation to God and God's revealed Law. It was a rather cartoonish vision by today's standards, but it seemed good enough then, and a religious education was a *complete* education. Today, however, in the West we have changed over to a new *empirical* way of describing and theorizing the world, which gives us much more compli-cated ideas about human nature. Since the 1950s, mass higher education, mass travel and communications, and ubiquitous high technology have gradually come to involve almost everybody in the new worldview. We need it for our jobs: Homer himself works in a nuclear power plant. And so our old religious and moral traditions have faded away, and nothing can resuscitate them.

That is why a tiny handful of us are not liberal, but radical, theologians. We say that the new culture is so different from anything that existed in the past that religion has to be completely reinvented. Unfortunately, the new style of religious thinking that we are trying to introduce is so queer and so new that most people have great difficulty in recognising it as religion at all.

Here is an example. Trying once again to produce a short, clear sum-mary of my own outlook, I recently wrote down my personal Creed. You'll think it very odd until I explain it. It is in five articles, four being about true religion and one about faith.

A CREED

1. True religion is your own voice, if you can but find it.
2. True religion is in every sense to *own* one's own life.
3. True religion is the pure solar affirmation of life, 'in full acknowledgement of its utter gratuitousness, its contingency, its transience, and even its nothingness'.
4. True religion is productive, value-realising action in the public world.
5. Faith is not a matter of holding onto anything. Faith is simply a letting-go. It floats free.

The first point to be made about this creed is that it makes no claims about any 'supernatural' or 'metaphysical' entities supposedly existing out there. Of course it doesn't: everything in the world of human life is transient and contingent, and always subject to changing human inter-pretations. We know nothing but the passing show of human life. That's all there is. We have to give up any idea of something purely objective and unchanging that underlies the world. It follows that a religious creed should no longer take the form of a declaration of allegiance to something out there, and I have to confess that I have entirely abandoned the old realistic-dogmatic way of thinking. There's nothing out there: there isn't anything but the disorderly flux of experience and the struggle of human language to build and maintain a tolerably stable and habitable world out of it. So religion today must follow ethics, and become autonomous—which in effect means seeing religion as a creative human activity, a way of adapting ourselves to life. Religion will become 'Protestantism-squared': it will be about our personal *style*—about the way we commit ourselves to the lifeworld in general, and to our own lives in particular. Religion, I say, is to be about the way you commit yourself to your own living and your life-task. Religion is about deciding what *you* are going to make of your own life. Life is all there is, and your life is all you have.

Article 1 therefore says that true religion is your own voice. I am sorry to have to risk causing offence, but I now reject all ready-made religious beliefs outright. Instead, I admit that I am pure heretic: I hold that true religion is now very close to art. Like a young artist, the religious person must struggle to find her own voice. She's trying to find the religious idiom through which she can best live her own life and become herself

and at ease with herself. We must therefore frame *our own* religious out-
looks and shape *our own* religious lives, and you will perhaps find—as
I have found—that when we are *in extremis* and getting close to death,
then the only religious beliefs that can help us at all are ones that we have
made for ourselves. That's pure and beautiful heresy: the only truth for
you is a truth that you have made up for yourself because it suits you, and
have tested out in your own life until it has become a part of you. Thus I
believe. Religion is a path to selfhood, and it comes out a bit different for
each one of us.

Article 2 is about owning one's own life, which means both acknowl-
edging it and assuming full responsibility for planning and running it. You
are your own life. Your personal identity is not a secret thing hidden inside
you: it is your lived life and the roles you play. Thus your commitment to
life and to the task of becoming yourself has to be read as the task of fully
appropriating one's own life and assuming full personal responsibility for
it. Here I reject the traditional idea that there is great virtue in obedience
to religious law and to the direction of religious superiors. Instead I join
all those young people who would rather die than put up with an arranged
marriage or any career or life-path chosen for them by someone else. In
traditional Christianity the demand for radical personal religious freedom
has always been condemned as deeply sinful, but I think we must now
insist upon it. One must choose one's own life, *both* making it one's own
and seeking fully to express oneself in it. One must *come out* in one's own
life.

Article 3 of my creed says that true religion is the pure solar affirmation
of life. We don't look for any incorruptible eternal world. We don't look for
absolutes. We say an all-out yes to our present life just as it is, gratuitous,
contingent, transient. ('Solar' means all-out and holding nothing back,
like the sun.) Of course our lives are fleeting and objectively 'meaningless'
but we can and we must *give* them meaning by the passion with which we
commit ourselves to life. We'll pass, but something of that passion will live
on and be remembered. It alone gives worth to life and to all the things
of life.

Talk of solar living brings us close to the biological use of the word 'life.'
Struggling for solarity brings us closer to other living things, and may fill
us with an overflowing love for them. So at least it is with me.

Which brings me to Article 4: True religion is productive value-
realising action in the public world. In the new age we have to do for ourselves what God used to do for us. In Genesis God's language creates light
and orders the world. Today it is *our* language that runs all over the chaos

of experience and makes all things intelligible—that is, bright and beauti-ful. *We* make the world. Similarly, as in Genesis God looks at what God has made and sees that it is good, so we collectively can look at what we have built up and see that it is good.

A favourite example of mine is a good modern illustrated bird book. The labour of thousands of ornithologists over the past two centuries has been sifted and accumulated to build up this beautiful and highly accurate inventory of the birds of our country or region. Before the Enlightenment they had nothing even approaching this. Not everything in the modern world is wrong and ugly. On the contrary, by a huge collective endeavour we have already made our world and our lives much more worked up, elaborated, and precious than ever they were in the past. And everyone, by the way they commit themselves to their own little corner of the world or of life, can and should contribute something to the work. I call this 'the ethics of value creation' or of 'world-building'. We should seek to build a world that looks as if it is 'divinely', or disinterestedly, loved.

Finally, Article 5 is about faith. For centuries faith has been fighting a slow, losing rearguard action, and it has got into the habit of seeing itself as clinging to what remains of various old 'certainties'. Orthodox faith has become like a very old person who is fearful, unable to change, and clutching at whatever is old and familiar. It demands external support—guardrails, bedrock, foundations. However, no such fixed eternal support is available, nor is it what we actually need. What faith needs is simply the confidence to forget personal anxiety and float free, enjoying life in the face of life's contingency. In the living of our lives, as in our science, anything is indeed possible, but we don't need to take all possibilities equally seriously all the time. We have to pick up the habit of selecting those few hypotheses about what may happen that are worth taking seriously or worth checking out, and then we should give them due consideration. The rest we should airily dismiss, and just get on with our lives. The truly 'solar' person understands that personal life is not really thinkable *at all* except against a background of contingency. Contingency as such is not an enemy; it is a condition of our life, and in particular of our freedom. We should not allow it to frighten us. We should affirm it, dancing out over it, and so turning hap into happiness. That is 'solarity'—the art of turning mere hap into eternal happiness by faith. And such faith is entirely rational. It conquers anxiety and helps us to rejoice in life, as the New Testament says, 'While we have time'. I feel a sense of eschatological urgency. Life is short: I haven't long, so I must rejoice in it while I can.

So much for my creed. Elsewhere I have pointed out that this very simple outline can be set against several different backgrounds, and fleshed out in many different vocabularies:

1. I have argued that it has already become the ordinary person's new religion—an autonomous *religion of life* that is demonstrably built into the idioms of today's ordinary language.[3]

2. In our post-metaphysical and naturalistic age, my creed might be defended as *Philosophy's Own Religion*.[4] It appears as such in postmodern French philosophy.

3. Alternatively, it can be presented as a new, post-ecclesiastical or 'kingdom' form of Christianity, that simply takes a step or two further the tradition of Kierkegaard, Bultmann, and Christian existentialism.[5] Thoroughly internalized commitment to God becomes commitment to existence, which in turn becomes commitment to our life now, the final goal of religion being just this return into simple immediacy.

4. My creed can also be interpreted as a layperson's version of Japanese Buddhism, perhaps especially in the Soto Zen tradition of Dogen.[6]

Thus the expressivist, self-outing, self-giving, and immediate religion of life that I am describing can be seen as the common outlook upon which several different traditions, each with its own distinctive vocabulary, are converging today in our globalized, postmodern times. Today we are giving up forever the idea that there is a privileged vocabulary that belongs exclusively to a particular community, which on that account controls access to salvation. No! Nobody has an exclusive franchise. There is no privileged vocabulary. Eternal happiness is available to all. It is easy to find, and ordinary language proves that the common people find it on their own *easily*, without any special help from any priesthood or academy. I sometimes call this 'Linux theology'. Truth is just sitting there, in public, and available for anyone who wants to use it. If you want to tweak it or add a little to it, you can do so. Why not? Truth is free: you don't have to bow down to anyone or pay anyone for it. Truth is common property.

We may also call what I am proposing 'democratic theology', a phrase that draws attention to a striking shift in thought. In the nineteenth and early twentieth centuries there was a belief that Great Men made everything. The makers of dictionaries showed how words should be used by quoting canonical writers. Great Men were the masters of language. They also made history, and 'religious geniuses' created religions. But in the most recent dictionaries we see that nowadays it is not Great Men but the common speech of ordinary people that has come to be seen as the principal site of linguistic innovation. Literary gems from Great Writers have become much less prominent, and instead the new dictionaries give long lists of the kind of stock phrases from ordinary language that professional writers usually look down upon. These phrases show that *ordinariness is also creative*.

We are in the midst of a big process of democratization. We are beginning to see the production of all meaning and of truths of every kind as something that comes about, not by Great Men laying down the law, but simply through the everyday conversation of humanity. I am extending this idea to religion and morality, saying that we must give up the idea that in these areas we should look up to any special and exalted Mouthpiece of Truth. No! On the contrary, we should give up all ideas of revelation and all ideas of traditional authority, and instead look for truth in the midst of common life and in the voices of ordinary people. We don't have to search for truth: it is already here amongst us. I first put forward these ideas nearly five years ago now, and so far there has been little understanding and no serious discussion of them, but I persist in saying that truth in philosophy, religion, and morality is public and easy to find. It is for everybody, and the method of enquiry that involves listening to the changing use of ordinary language delivers it to us much more easily and quickly than applying to any of the traditional authorities. I now see the new religion as one that doesn't need to be strenuously propagated. It crops up and propagates itself spontaneously, among the people and all the time.

To understand this process of religious democratization is to understand why in ordinary language in the past generation or two the stock of 'organised religion' has fallen steadily, and the stock of 'spirituality' has risen correspondingly. 'Organised religion' taught us to think of itself as uniquely possessing a large 'deposit' of unchanging and compulsory copyrighted truth, which its own authorities certify to us. That's an idea we are fast abandoning. 'Spirituality' teaches us to think instead of religion and morality as human and changing. Everyone is a lifelong pilgrim, everyone is trying to work out the religious style or idiom that's right for her. We all of us develop and project out our own personal religion, and there's no harm in that. People who are committed to one of the great traditions of organised religion, and people involved with academic theology, usually scorn the new spirituality, saying that it is hopelessly irrational, amateurish, and self-indulgent. Well, maybe—though I wouldn't describe the professional apologists of organised religion as being themselves paragons of rationality, either. And in any case, whether you like 'spirituality' or not, it is the future, and my creed can be seen as trying to give this new kind of personally evolved religion or 'principled heresy' a rationale.

I have made a bold claim. I have suggested that we in the modern West are finally abandoning the old 'dogmatic' vision of the world and are moving over to a new outlook which I have elsewhere called 'Empty radical humanism'.[7] To put it with brutal brevity, there is no permanent objective reality: there is only the endless human debate through which we struggle, out of the chaos of experience, to build a habitable scene for our common life. Religion in this new era has to take a new form: it is the task of finding and adopting the personal philosophy of life and lifestyle through which we can best live, become ourselves, love life, and enhance the value of our own corner of the common human world. We need to find each of us a personal way of committing ourselves, with all the religious intensity we can muster, to life in general and to our own lives in particular. So far as we can succeed in this aim, we can help to make the whole lifeworld more valuable and make it a bit easier for future humans to rejoice in life and to live well. Your spirituality, then, is your personal lifestyle and life-project, and your contribution within the greater project of humanity as a whole.

That seems straightforward, and even rational. It is rational for each of us to seek for himself the outlook and to cultivate the habits that will help him to make the best of the human situation, and be happy. So far so good. But how is my defence of the modern vogue for spirituality to be reconciled with what we actually find in the bookshops? Every big general stockholding bookshop nowadays has sections that are variously labelled 'Body, Mind and Spirit' or 'Phenomena', or 'Spirituality'. And what do we find on the shelves there?—An avalanche of terminally self-indulgent tosh. Popular spirituality bears the same sort of relation to mainstream public scientific knowledge as fringe medicine bears to orthodox science-based medicine. Pop spirituality is 'fringe' or 'alternative'—and we should steer well clear of it. It is a jumble of fuzzy language, anecdotal evidence, wish-fulfilment, and the sort of ideas that in ordinary language people introduce after the phrase, 'I like to think that . . .'.

What went wrong? I accept—and insist—that there is indeed a large-scale religious shift currently taking place. It is taking us away from the great disciplinary religious institutions with their ready made creeds and towards a new conception of religion that demands a high degree of personal autonomy. People need to work out their own religious *style*—their own way of life and path to selfhood, their own way of loving life and cherishing their bit of the world, and somehow their own way of saying yes to life just as it is. But this quest for a valid personal religion certainly does not have to take the form of a compensatory fantasy. On the contrary, it can only really satisfy us if it is firmly based on a cool recognition of the facts of the human condition: we are alone, everything passes away, we'll die, and there is no magic formula or specially provided way out of all this. *All this* is outsideless, and there is no supernatural escape route or consolation. But by faith and love and commitment to life it is possible to turn the pure hap of life into eternal happiness. I call the trick 'solar living', and *that* is true religion. There is no other way.

From all this you will understand why I don't just admit, but insist, that religion today has to become beliefless. There is nothing out there to believe in or to hope for. Religion therefore has to become an immediate and deeply felt way of relating yourself to life in general and your own life in particular. Live it out, hard, and I promise that you'll find it works.

This explains why it is that although I strongly sympathize with the general movement from 'organised religion' to 'spirituality', I regard it as essential that we make ourselves very unpopular by being severely critical of soppy fringe spirituality, and by telling people that they should have nothing to do with it. Under the old régime, the religious life used to begin with something called the Purgative Way, which was designed to purge the mind of illusions. Modern spirituality still needs something like that, and knows it, for of course every human being knows and has always known the basic facts of the human condition: everything passes, everything is chancy, we'll die, and because everything is outsidelessly this way there is not and there can't be any kind of magical escape or consolation. Everyone knows all these things, and everyone therefore knows that fringe religion is nonsense and that the old kind of organised religion with its ready-made creed was only a temporary stopgap. Now it has broken down, and we all of us know in our hearts that it is time to move on to the fully grown-up kind of religion that awaits us next. It starts from and it clings to a cool and unflinching recognition of the truth of the human condition, and, nevertheless, it *still* wants to say an all-out yes to life—right up to one's last breath.

What, however, is its relation to the Judaeo-Christian tradition, whose highly problematic future is much debated at present? It must be obvious that I personally think that the ecclesiastical Christianity that we have received from the past is now in precipitous and final decline. Its theology, which was chiefly systematized by St Augustine of Hippo in his book *The City of God*, involved a hugely large-scale and long-termist cosmological myth of Creation, Fall, and Redemption, and a highly illiberal and precritical politics of truth. Today, the great medieval doctrine system—even in the refurbished version that has reached us *via* Calvin and Karl Barth—is way beyond any possibility of rehabilitation; and as for the politics of truth that represses religious creativity and tries to bully us all into passive conformity, it is morally unendurable. Sooner or later, we must either break it or break with it, before it breaks us.

I am not suggesting, though, that we should or even *can* break with Christianity altogether. It is too much a part of us, our world, and our values. Personally, I still admire the original Jesus, and I see Christianity as the religion that is always coming down, from God to humans, from the world above into this present world, and from mystical rapture into everyday life. In Christianity God himself is a secular humanist, for he becomes man in the world, and everything comes back in the end to the world of human life and human relationships. Christianity still is and always was trying to develop in the way I've been describing: religion, it said from the first, is made for man, and not man for religion.[8] That's non-realism in a nutshell.

Accordingly I have still not entirely given up hope that there may yet be another reformation of Christianity, which will need to press on with and radicalize the great tradition of Luther, Kierkegaard, Bultmann, and Christian existentialism. Along these lines, as I have tried to show, those themes in Christianity that are most precious may yet have a future. But as I have insisted, it is vital that we give up the old politics of truth—and especially the community politics. We must abandon the idea that *we* are the chosen people, *we* use the right vocabulary, and *we* alone have privileged access to eternal salvation. If the human race is to have a future we must give up all forms of nationalism and ethnocentrism—and most especially the religious forms of these ideas. So my future reformation will require Christianity to give up its own identity and its own claim to a privileged status. And that is the last, the most difficult, and the most necessary sacrifice.

2

THE END OF DOGMATIC THINKING

Influenced by the great success and prestige of the Swiss Protestant theologian Karl Barth (1886–1968), many young academic theologians, until recently, still dreamt of reviving something called 'systematic theology', or 'church dogmatics'. I have known several such people. At the outset of their careers they were full of hope: they thought that they knew what Christian faith is, they thought they could see how it might be possible to articulate its intellectual content in systematic form, and they were all going to contribute to the great work.

The years have passed, but the books have not come. Indeed, the prospect of their ever being written is now so remote as to be right out of sight. What might be their sources—the Bible and the Christian tradition? Both look far more loose-knit, diverse, and inconclusive than they did in Karl Barth's relatively innocent days. Neither speaks with a single voice: neither ever did, not even at the very beginning. You can maintain that the Bible is or in some sense contains 'the Word of God', and that it teaches—or 'witnesses to'—a systematic theology, but only if you are as completely cut off from any serious study of it as an Evangelical is. As for the Christian tradition, it is an unedifying jumble and a dusty relic of a world now lost forever. Only two major Christian dogmas were ever defined by the (more or less) undivided church with (more or less) general agreement, namely the dogmas of the Incarnation and the Trinity, and both of them are problematic because by modern critical standards they are not in fact 'scriptural' in the way they claim to be. Otherwise, we do not actually have clear and agreed definitions of the doctrines of God, the Resurrection, the Atoning death of Christ, and so on.

How then is systematic or dogmatic theology to be written? If it is to be worked up from primary sources—namely, the Bible, 'the Fathers', and official church statements—and if it needs to be fully consistent with all those sources, then the work of construction cannot be done in any rigorous way; or at least it cannot be done in such a way as to command general consent. The sources are themselves too much in dispute, and at odds with each other. The best a young theologian can aim to produce is something of the same status as an imaginative writer's retelling of the Arthuriad, perhaps in such a work as T.H. White's *The Once and Future King*. But exactly what sort of truth and what degree of authority could be claimed for such an imaginative fiction,[1] and what would be the use of it? Who would read it? We cannot say. It is not surprising that prudent young theologians nowadays confine themselves to writing historical theology. It offers a short and easy way to applause and preferment.

The melancholy fact is that today Christian doctrine is dead. We cannot agree on how its statements can be generated and justified, and still less can we see what useful work they can do. We cannot find any place for these statements on the map of modern knowledge, and they appear to be meaningless.

For example, one still from time to time hears people say that 'God made us', or that 'We are all the children of God'. Now, after half a century of striking discoveries in Kenya and the neighbouring lands along the course of the Rift Valley, we have built a large quantity of evidence and a rich, complicated scientific story about human origins. During the same period, modern molecular biology has also developed rapidly, and we are now developing extremely detailed accounts of how human and other primate bodies work. With all this in mind, the current scientific story offers the one and only serious answer on the market to questions about human origins, and how we have come to be what we now are. Its main outlines are familiar to everyone: so why are people still declaring sententiously that 'God made us'? What can they possibly mean? What event do they have in mind, who was around to observe and report this event, and what evidence can we find of its occurrence?

The statement that 'God made us', despite its frequent use, seems to have no meaning. I don't see how we are to explain it, justify it, or relate it to the now-very-rich picture of human nature and origins offered by modern biological anthropology. I cannot imagine ever again being able to bring myself to talk that kind of talk. And, unfortunately, virtually the whole of religious doctrine is now in the same position.

Take the case of the belief that someone has ascended into heaven. In a loose sort of way, we can and do refer cheerfully to the ascensions of Elijah, Enoch, Mary, the Prophet Muhammad (blessed be he), and the proverbial Chinaman who is hoisted up to heaven by his pigtail. We know about these old stories, and they are quite amusing. But what is it dogmatically to believe that one such story—perhaps, that of the Ascension of Christ—is seriously and dogmatically just true; so seriously that one takes the trouble annually to observe a feast that commemorates this great event? How would you explain the mechanics of the ascension to a space scientist, and what makes it religiously important to *us* that we should believe such things today?

For twenty years and more I have argued that although when they are interpreted realistically the propositions of Christian dogma now make no sense at all, we can make good sense of them if we interpret them in a non-realistic and properly religious way. Thus the belief that God created the world *ex nihilo* makes no sense at all if we interpret it as saying that a superbeing sitting in eternity spoke a word, and the universe instantly exploded into being; and that this account of God as bringing about the Big Bang needs only to be hooked onto the side of the current scientific theory, as an optional extra for believers. That account, I say, is grotesque; but there is a non-realistic interpretation of belief in God as Creator that is religious and does make perfect sense. You believe in the creation of the world out of nothing if, all the time, you receive and you treat your own life as a pure gift continually renewed. Someone who has just emerged from a serious illness and a major operation may feel that from now on all life is a bonus and is to be accepted in a spirit of gratitude. That is exactly right: indeed we should all of us live like that —and *that* is what it is to believe in 'creation out of nothing'. My life is pure gift, with no giver.

One should interpret the statement about Christ, that 'he ascended into heaven', in a similar way. You believe in the ascension if Jesus has ascended and is enthroned, 'in your heart' i.e. ethically, in your life. When you interpret the ascension in a non-realistic and ethical way—that is, in terms of the way it should work out in your living—then you understand correctly the *religious* point of the belief. Religious beliefs are not metaphysical speculations, but guides to living.[2] They influence the way we see life, feel about life, value life.

By interpreting Christian dogma non-realistically along these lines I tried over a twenty-year period to save the old vocabulary (or most of it), and at the same time to renew the old religion. But I failed completely. The faithful could not contemplate giving up the traditional dogmatic kind of belief and thinking, and replacing it with a more ethical and religious kind of thinking. They were united in rejecting my whole case out of hand, and in clinging to their traditional realism. In the case of the Resurrection, for example, the faithful have seen their Frankenstein films and they just *know* that to believe in a resurrection is to believe that a corpse has been given a sharp electric shock and has come back to life. The mystery of the Resurrection is the mystery of a resuscitated corpse, and that is that. The emptiness of the Tomb is the essence of the matter. I might try feebly quoting St Paul, and say that you count as believing in the Resurrection if, and only if, you are yourself actually living a new and risen life; but I had no hope of being listened to by people for whom the Resurrection is a science-fiction event in the remote past. The faithful *know* that the true doctrine of the resurrection is the one that was laid down by the fathers of fundamentalism at Niagara a century ago, and nothing will shift them. For the faithful, their own brand of literalism is 'traditional' and 'orthodox', and they will never budge. My attempt to revive a more seriously *religious* interpretation of Christianity is of no interest to them, no doubt because they are not and never were very interested in religion just as such. What they are interested in is factional infighting, and power over others. That's all they've *ever* cared about. They illustrate very well the ancient nexus in Christianity between truth and power that began with St Paul, and I have no option but to concede that they have easily won the power struggle, and will go on winning it. They are very good at it: it's what they specialize in. They are now in the driving seat, they control meaning and therefore they control truth. The Gospel is what they say it is, and no other view will gain a hearing.

The upshot of all this is that my attempt to save much of traditional Christian vocabulary by interpreting it in a consistently non-realistic and ethical way has failed. I never had any prospect of being taken seriously. The neoconservative power-men (for they are indeed virtually all of them males) have taken over and cannot now be dislodged. It is best therefore to relinquish to them the vocabulary that we cannot hope to wrest from them. At the same time I should also admit that the whole vocabulary of Christian dogmatics and the way of thinking involved are now completely meaningless to me, and I cannot do anything with them. It has long been hijacked for use in the spiritual power games of the various sorts of neo-conservatives, traditionalists, and fundamentalists. For them, the phrases of standard Christian doctrine are now simply laws that they want to see enforced, and passwords to be used as loyalty tests. Doctrine is law. It defines the community: it has a disciplinary function. For the neoconservatives, this objectified and legalistic understanding of 'belief' is sufficient. But it is not enough for me, so I must withdraw and leave the neoconservatives to enjoy their triumph.

* * * * *

The position just described is an odd end to the history of Christianity, but it was implicit from the beginning. Sometimes in a restaurant our meal is long delayed, and we become uneasily aware of mysterious ructions going on behind the scenes. We ask the most authoritative-looking of the waiters for an explanation, and he tries to spin a story. As time passes and still the meal doesn't arrive, the story becomes longer and ever less plausible. We ask someone else what's happening, but this leads to the production of another story and then to conflict between rival interpretations.

So it was in the early history of Christianity. Jesus was probably a teacher of wisdom, and perhaps also a healer. His miserable death was at first presented simply as the unjust martyrdom of an innocent man and as a case of severe suffering nobly borne. Some hoped he might yet be vindicated and claimed that he himself had hoped for vindication, whether before or very soon after his dying. Stories grew that interpreted his death as a sacrifice by which a new covenant had been inaugurated, and promised his speedy return in glory. But why was his return so long delayed? A theory was needed: the struggle for leadership in the early community became a struggle between rival theologies. And so the classic Christian nexus between truth and power was established: for the one who wins the power struggle gets to define and to embody 'orthodoxy'. And so it remains to this day: truth is controlled by power. Those who have won the struggle for spiritual power in the community naturally regard as 'truth' whatever is in their own interests. They canonize a theological story that legitimates themselves. Their theological interpretation is God's revelation, and you'd better believe it. They've won, and you either submit or you get out.

It is because of this long history that to this day in all the formerly Christian countries of the West people assume that a religious person is 'a believer', one of 'a flock' that accepts the teaching of a leader: that a religion is 'a creed', and that the most honest and admirable religion is the one in which people are the most unanimous in holding a large, defining set of doctrinal beliefs, beliefs that equip the faithful with stock answers to all the questions they are allowed to ask. Holding lots of clearly defined beliefs is reckoned to be good for your soul, and religious bodies that do not concern themselves very much with enforcing dogmas are ridiculed. They are considered woolly: they don't believe anything very much.

So it is said. But in the long run this doctrinal legalism, and the general assumption that in religion truth is to be defined and enforced by power and power alone, is profoundly self-destructive. It has already destroyed Protestantism, and bids fair soon to destroy Catholicism as well. In the case of Protestantism, the leading reformers were well aware of the slow decline of metaphysics since the late thirteenth century, and they decided to reject philosophy and rely entirely upon the authority of the Bible. But then during the nineteenth century secular knowledge expanded enormously, biblical criticism developed, and the whole of Christian apologetics crashed. Inevitably, the churches decided that if Christian doctrine was no longer demonstrably true *de facto*, they could at least ensure that it was true *de jure*. If the true faith couldn't be defined rationally, it must instead be defined and enforced *as law*. The elders of the church must be vigilant in sniffing out and extirpating heresy in their midst. So Protestantism gradually turned first into puritanism and then into fundamentalism, and even in my own once-great church the exercise of doctrinal authority has become gradually more overbearing and nonrational. We are now threatened with a revival of trials for heresy. Under these conditions, the churches have gradually ceased to be seriously concerned about religion. Instead, they function as theatres in which spiritual power over others is gathered, displayed, and exercised. In brief, churches now exist to provide their own leaders with the power bases they crave, and for no other purpose.

Here, I am concerned only to argue that we must entirely abandon the dogmatic kind of thinking, and the dogmatic conception of what religious belief is. Most of all, we must break with the notion that those in power have the right to define and enforce religious truth. We need to put a lot of clear blue water between us and people who think in such terms.

3

I have been aware for many years of not holding any religious beliefs—at least not in the popular sense of what religious beliefs are, and what it is to hold them. This is not surprising: forty years in the academy makes you that way. An habitually critical way of thinking that is forever questioning meanings, scrutinizing finely balanced arguments pro and con, and digging up the foundations must in due course produce a completely demythologized and emptied state of mind—cool and benignly interested, but without any sacred, unquestionable, and permanent principles or attachments. On the contrary, everything is always open to question—including the principle just stated in the first half of this sentence.

Academics in the arts subjects end up surprisingly uncommitted. It's their version of the scientific attitude. But it creates an odd paradox: theology becomes the one subject whose practitioners are in constant danger of finding themselves becoming demythologized right out of their subject, and then being told by everyone that they have a duty to resign. The corollary is that you can be a theologian in good standing only for so long as you are not very good because you don't yet see your subject clearly and in an up-to-date way. You may plan to survive the difficulty by adopting the time-honoured strategies of being evasive, or sticking to history, and so avoiding ever actually having to come clean about your own personal views. But you cannot help but feel a little uncomfortable about the paradox: an academic must seek full, transparent understanding, but when you fully understand religion you are no longer a 'believer'.

I want to escape from this dilemma by maintaining that there is nothing at all odd about being a highly religious person without holding any religious beliefs. It is becoming almost the norm today, and not least so among philosophers. I have elsewhere quoted the late Ernest Gellner saying in private conversation that although he was no sort of religious believer, 'I do have a religious attitude to life'. Wittgenstein, in a rather similar vein, may have been alluding to his own consciousness of being part Jewish when he declared that: 'I can't help approaching every problem from a religious point of view'. It was common in his lifetime to draw a contrast between the metaphysics of vision in Greek thought and the metaphysics of hearing and language in Jewish thought. The Greek tends to see religiousness in terms of emptied, objective, visual contemplation of ideal beauty—perhaps in the form of an image of Apollo. The very word *theory* was originally associated with religious spectacle. In sharp contrast, the Jew puts the sense of hearing first, and hearing is very much more inward than sight. We see out there, but we hear inside our heads. Think of the telephone, or the personal stereo. Spoken language is intensely intimate and commanding: it is prior to us, speaks us, speaks in us and to us. And when Wittgenstein says that although as a philosopher he obviously doesn't hold and cannot possibly hold any dogmatic beliefs, he nevertheless cannot help approaching every problem from the religious point of view, he seems to be saying that 'the religious point of view' is a way of thinking that is acutely aware of language, of the claims of the ethical, and of the way the self is always involved. The scientific attitude tries to leave out the self, or reduce it to being no more than a rather abstract ideal observer which looks into the world from a viewpoint that is not itself part of the world. But philosophy cannot try systematically to leave out the self and its interest in that way. On the contrary, philosophy is a quest for a kind of all-round understanding, or 'wisdom', that of course *must* include the self, the way it is placed in the world and in language, and its interest. In the philosophical quest we have to include the self because we are looking for our own final happiness, in a sense that science never pretends to match.

In these considerations Wittgenstein shows again his debt to Schopenhauer. In their first origin philosophy and religion more or less coincide. Both begin with awe and wonder at the world and the human condition. What are we, what can we know, what is there for us? What is thinking, what is language, and what kind of happiness, or at least resignation and acceptance of the way things are, can we hope to attain? What has happened in our own late-modern period is that scientific and critical thinking have gradually eroded and demythologized away all dogmatic belief, gradually leading us full circle back to the days when philosophy and religion more or less coincided. One is conscious of trying to make a new beginning, and of looking afresh at the old great questions of life.

Religion without beliefs, then, is not a freakish eccentricity. On the contrary, it is more like a return of innocence. We discover a liking for the pre-Socratic philosophers, and enjoy recapturing a little of the overwhelming immediacy and force with which people at the beginning of our tradition experienced the great questions.[1] In my philosophical thought-experiments I enjoy trying to confront, as belieflessly as possible, the 'fountaining' or forthcoming of Be-ing from moment to moment; the passing of time; the gathering or collection of the self as one wakes up and 'comes to oneself' in the morning; the taking of small risks to find out how I really feel about everything's contingency; and so on. That's religion now: the attempt to meet, feel, negotiate with, come to terms with, and accept the great ambient conditions of our life. One is coming to terms with It All, or existence, or life, or everything, or whatever one may prefer to call it; and if at this primitive level there is any difference between philosophy and religion, it is that in religion we feel more urgently the pressure of a personal need to find one's own *modus vivendi*. I want a deal and I want it fast.[2] When I feel I've made my deal, I am filled with that special intense joy that is religion's great reward. I've arrived, I'm there.

Alternatively, in philosophy the element of speculative curiosity is rather stronger, and we may feel willing to stay longer with the questions, turning them over and over and watching their shapes and relationships change. The joy of philosophy is the pleasure—perhaps even the sense of mastery—that we get when during the long, slow mulling-over of the questions we are suddenly struck by a brand new and genuinely good angle, metaphor, or argument. Briefly we have seen **It All make sense**, we have been **where It's At**, we have glimpsed the top. A few moments like that are enough to make an entire life worthwhile.[3]

These special rewards and moments of happiness that we may be lucky enough to enjoy in religion or philosophy cannot be sought directly. They come only as an occasional and unlooked-for bonus, and must not be invoked in a philosophical argument. They 'prove' nothing. But many people think otherwise. They want to equate beliefless, immediate religiousness with religious experience, and they believe that a mystical kind of religious experience—which they usually read as some kind of intuitive awareness of the divine—has always been and still is widespread among human beings in all cultures. By studying and theorizing this kind of experience; they think that we can hope to develop a genuinely empirical science of religion.[4]

I want to say, thanks—but no, thanks. These 'religious experiences'— like the philosophical experiences, too—are purely natural events in our psychological history. We shouldn't make the mistake of supposing them to be cognitive, and we shouldn't try to build anything upon them. In philosophy it is a very good rule that one should always be deeply suspicious of appeals to intuition, and indeed of appeal to anything outside language. If you want to strengthen a proposition in philosophy, you must produce an argument in support of it; that is, you must produce something else that is *also* propositional. But don't try to get outside language, for appeal to an alleged intuitive knowledge of something extra-linguistic is *never* a good move in philosophy. To put the point sharply and provocatively, philosophy just *is* non-realism. I mean that since the time of Kant and Hegel modern philosophy has gradually come to acknowledge that knowledge and truth are not given to us from above. We ourselves, have been and are the only framers of all our knowledge. We made it all up. Furthermore, since propositional 'thought' is dependent upon language, all our knowledge is constructed within language—and therefore within the ongoing, ever-changing human conversation that we call history. Thus the typically realist attempt to anchor our knowledge objectively, by trying to hook it onto something permanent that sits outside language, rests upon a mistake. Since knowledge as such is a human invention, and is language-dependent, of course there ain't anything knowable outside and independent of language that can justify a particular philosophical claim.

Along such lines as these, the close modern study of religion and of philosophy must eventually lead us to a non-realistic or 'noncognitive' account of religious belief, and to non-realism in philosophy generally. But as I have been insisting, it should not lead us to think that we must abandon religion because we have suddenly discovered that 'there's nothing in it'. On the contrary, I am arguing that it leads us back to an innocent, beliefless confrontation with the great questions of life and to the hope of a new beginning.

4

I have been suggesting that during the late eighteenth century the modern project of systematic critical thinking, first launched by René Descartes, became much more fully self-critical in the Critical Philosophy of Kant. Its effect in the long run has been to make us much more aware of the extent to which we ourselves always have been and still are the only makers of language, meaning, truth, and our whole world-picture—including, be it added at once, all our ideas about ourselves. The new outlook may be called 'Empty radical humanism', with the emphasis on the word *Empty*, because we must not make the mistake of supposing that what has happened is merely a Copernican revolution that turns everything inside-out and replaces the old theocentric outlook with a new anthropocentric outlook. No: the new outlook, which Hegel begins to describe, brings everything down into a beginningless, endless, and radically outsideless process of symbolic exchange—history, the human conversation—through which and within which everything comes to be and passes away. Everything passes, everything is a transient construct, everything is disputable and negotiable. We produce everything within our talk, including, of course, all our ideas about ourselves. We come, and we go.

After the publication of the first edition of Kant's *Critique of Pure Reason* (1781), it took only about sixty years for Karl Marx to reach the end of metaphysics—the end, that is, of a conception of the task of the philosophy that went back to Parmenides and Plato, and saw the philosopher as looking beyond the world of appearances to a timeless intelligible

31

real world, an order of reason that exists prior to and independently of human beings. In this ancient picture, in which Kant himself is still to some degree caught up, philosophy is realism. Human reason is not a mere biological survival-adaptation, but is taken to be objective. There is reason out there and there is eternal, *a priori* truth out there. The philosopher is the anatomist of the whole world of *a priori* truths: he lays down the foundations for every branch of knowledge.

After Kant, we slowly began to see that we ourselves put up all that stuff. *We* invented logic, *we* invented arithmetic and geometry. There is no mathematical heaven beyond the bright blue sky. Philosophy nowadays is non-realism. And this great change of outlook quickly began to influence religious thought as well. The whole mighty apparatus of organized religion—creed, scripture, rituals, iconography, priestly authority, and so on—had all seemed to be objective. It claimed divine authority. It ruled society, it generated Dante Alighieri's huge cosmology, it seemed to be overwhelmingly real. It was sacred, and you dared not touch it. But after Kant we began to see all of it as just an historically accumulated human creation, our own collective work of folk-art. *We* made all these institutions and stories that are sacred to us. With this realization tradition became demythologized and lost its old authority. Human religiousness began to free itself from its old dependence upon authority and supernatural belief. What was once a vast cosmology and a whole religion-based civilization gradually telescoped into a matter of one's personal choice of lifestyle. True religion? It is simply a way of owning and committing your life, and of saying an all-out solar yes to life in general. The old cosmic and objective stuff, the *mystique*, once functioned to give the church an aura of grandeur, but means little to us now. We can set it aside.

In the 1830s and 1840s a few people began to understand this enormous cultural shift. They were the young Hegelians, people like Feuerbach and Marx. It is not surprising that the idea began to dawn, first that Western thought was moving towards a certain consummation or fulfilment, and second that it was thereby coming full circle and returning into its own origin. Since antiquity, philosophy had moved out into metaphysics and objectification, and then since the fourteenth century it had gradually come back into immanence and human everydayness. Religion similarly had gone to the highest degree of institutionalization and objectification, with the construction of a large-scale sacred cosmology; but now the whole sacred realm had returned *via* the Protestant Reformation to the human lifeworld and into the heart of the individual believer. There had been a great cycle of objectification and return, expansion and contraction, dispersal and recollection, diastole and systole, the whole cycle having taken some twenty three centuries on one account (or twenty six centuries, if you preferred Nietzsche's version of the story, which started with Homer rather than with Parmenides).

The implication of this circular movement, first into metaphysics and long-termist disciplinary religion and then back into human everydayness, is that we today find ourselves in the same sort of position as people were in early Greece, between Homer and the pre-Socratic philosophers. The great disciplinary institutions have lost much of their old power, and the old supernatural world above us is gone. Above us now, as John Lennon excellently put it, there is 'only sky'. We are innocent and emptied—and we are therefore now able to meet the great questions of life, the founding questions of philosophy, with a clarity and head-on directness that have been impossible for over two millennia.

Very well: Are you with me so far? Then what exactly *are* the Great Questions of Life, about which we still hear a good deal nowadays? Where is there a convenient list of them?

There isn't, of course. The fact is that different writers give strikingly different accounts of what they suppose the great questions to be, the differences between them apparently reflecting their special personal concerns and interests.

Thus, in the English-speaking world, where philosophy is not highly regarded by the general public and 'religious thought' is regarded as an oxymoron, there is a tendency to encourage middle-aged celebrity scientists to set up as sages and pronounce upon the Ultimate Questions. Not surprisingly, we learn that the ultimate questions are, for example, 'How did the Universe first come into being?' 'How did life begin?' and 'How did human beings first appear on earth? What's special about us?' The great questions are thus seen as demands for stories about origins, and they are answered by reciting the current scientific narrative about each topic. The suggestion is that science is already beginning to develop a cosmic grand narrative that will one day fully replace the traditional stories of religion, and perhaps even of philosophy. So far as the great questions of life are real, answerable questions, science, and science alone, is going to answer them.

By contrast, the great philosopher Immanuel Kant was a Newtonian and a Protestant. He saw nature as a value-free zone and held that we must take a deterministic view of it. The life of the individual human being was a demanding, solitary pilgrimage through an unfriendly world, sustained by a decidedly shadowy faith in an ultimate vindication beyond death.

Given that general worldview, Kant saw the ultimate questions as being something like: 'What can I know?' 'What ought I to do?' and 'What may I hope?'[1] Here the individual seeks not scientific stories about origins, but personal support and reassurance of an ethical and philosophical kind. One needs to believe that life can be worthwhile, that sense can be made of it, and that there is something to look forward to.

A third example is supplied by Buddhism, whose great thought is about the ubiquity of human suffering and the possibility of finding a cure for suffering not in some sort of theoretical explanation of it, but simply by following the life-path laid down by the Buddha. In Buddhist teaching, therefore, the traditional philosophical great questions—about God and the creation of the world, about the human soul and so on—are expressly set aside and left undecided so that for the present we can deal with just the One Great Question and the strictly practical answer to it. The question is that of suffering, its ubiquity, its nature, and the remedy for it; and the answer is that one must without delay begin to walk along the noble eightfold path. When we have gone some way in the practice of Buddhism we may expect to find that the other great questions have effectively answered themselves by ceasing to trouble us and melting away. 'Just chill out', says Buddhism.

Our fourth example of a modern philosopher of life is Arthur Schopenhauer, who kept little statuettes of Kant and the Buddha on his desk. For him both philosophical thinking and religious thinking are ultimately driven by a sense of cosmic wonder, by dread at the thought of our own mortality, and by the urgent need to seek some kind of consolation and relief in the face of the unhappiness that plagues us. As he put it once: 'Life is a wretched business. I've decided to spend it trying to understand it'.[2] From the days of Parmenides to the time of Schelling and Schopenhauer it had just about invariably been assumed that the Real is One, perfect, and rationally coherent. But Schopenhauer boldly and bravely introduces the opposite thought, that noumenal reality—'the World as Will'—is permanently and irredeemably at odds with itself in a way that we find painfully reflected in our own deep psychology. Schopenhauer is left with no sure remedy for life's woes beyond gradually giving up our desire for life and finding some consolation in art and in philosophy.

In Schopenhauer we find an early illustration of the fundamental achievement of nineteenth-century thought, its ability to raise, question, and reject deep assumptions, long engrained. Schopenhauer was proto-evolutionist in outlook, and had a strong sense of the littleness of the human being and her thoughts in the face of the universe's vastness and violence. It's becoming clear that we can no longer just assume that reality is ultimately One and in some sense rational and ordered. We can't assume that there is some kind of harmony between thought and being, or between the way language is ordered and the way the world is ordered. This is getting serious, for now we see that we cannot assume that we know, or even *can* know, what the big questions are, or—better—we cannot assume that once we've got the questions right we can expect to find ready-made big answers to them sitting out there, waiting for us to come along and pick them up. Even to this day many or most scientists are metaphysical realists who naively assume that nature talks our language: we question nature, and nature returns ready-made answers already framed in our language and intelligible to us. Most convenient—but how *can* we assume this, after we have accepted that we ourselves are products of natural selection? Surely all we are entitled to conclude is that our sense organs and our thought processes have evolved to help us survive to reproduce. As a budding young philosopher wrote in the 1870s: 'Our truths are those illusions without which we cannot live'. He saw that when human reason becomes consistently critical about itself, in an age when we have been driven to accept a thoroughly naturalistic account of what human thinking is and how it has evolved, a major crisis of scepticism, and even nihilism, is upon us.[3]

If Darwinism is true, how were we poor talking animals ever able even to formulate it, much less to recognize its truth? Surely the very sentence, *Darwinism is true*, is reflexively paradoxical: for if Darwinism is true then the very notion of truth, as we have hitherto understood it, is dead. If Darwinism is true, then there is no truth, and therefore Darwinism can't be true (if, of course, I can even say *that*).

I am here talking, of course, about Nietzsche, our fifth example. He suddenly forces us to question the assumption upon which I have been conducting this discussion so far. We have supposed that the modern, self-critical, and fully enlightened human being, who lives after the end of metaphysics and after the end of the realistic, dogmatic kind of religious belief, is a person with a wonderfully open mind. His head is emptied and clear. He is going to be in a position—isn't he?—to see and formulate the great questions of life with perfect clarity and confidence.

It isn't as easy as that. Nietzsche saw better than anyone before him that at the moment when Enlightenment becomes complete *it destroys itself* and we are plunged into a crisis of nihilism. The upshot is that Nietzsche's philosophy changes the great questions radically. The one question he poses for us is: 'What is going to happen to our ideas of truth and value? How are we going to live with the implications *for ourselves* of the huge modern growth of critically tested empirical knowledge and scientific theory?' His answer is not easy. He holds that for 25 centuries and more we have been domesticated men, content to live within a ready-made framework. Now that framework is gone, eroded away by critical thinking (and ultimately by the strenuous Christian demand for inner truthfulness). We are going to have to become much more than people have been so far. We must learn to live by being creative: we must learn to say a consistent all-out Yes to life. We must create new truths, new gods, new values.

For a sixth example of a modern philosopher of life, and the way he sees the great questions, we turn now briefly to Nietzsche's most important successor, Martin Heidegger. We turn to him because Heidegger exemplifies the main ideas of this chapter more neatly than anyone else so far. He takes up the idea current since Hegel that Western thought has recently come to, or even gone rather past, its own 'end'. We have come full circle, and we feel an affinity with the pre-Socratic philosophers of antiquity. We need to make the turn to 'life', and to frame a new account of the human condition. Finally, we need a new formulation of the great questions of life; and because Heidegger is one of those philosophers who likes to see every major thinker as having just one great thought, he sums up his own account of the great questions in one, which he calls the Question of Being.

As Heidegger sees it, ever since Parmenides and Plato Western thought has tended to see real being as absolute: that is, as self-existent, one, timeless, and perfect. The whole empirical world of changeable, finite things in time has tended to be described as a realm of mere 'becoming', i.e., not *real* Being at all, for during the long centuries of Christian Platonism religion had encouraged us sharply to separate real Being from everything temporal. Real Being is timelessly self-existent, unchanging, and selfsame. That made God necessarily the only Real Being, and we taught ourselves systematically to devalue our own corruptible world and our own fragile lives. But then from Hegel onwards we began radically to historicize all reality, and this produced a violent reversal of outlook. Now *all* being is temporal. The flowing, intersubjective, historical human world, the world of becoming, is all there is. We have hitherto been taught to think of it as corrupt and unstable. Only by a constant exertion of the sustaining Will of God was created, finite being preserved from instantly collapsing into nothingness. But now we find ourselves obliged to rethink finite being—or perhaps we should call it be-ing, to remind ourselves that it is always temporal—and we have to find ways of loving it, trusting it, saying Yes to it, and affirming it, just as it is.

Heidegger seems always to have wished to avoid openly and finally repudiating his Catholic background, and when he speaks of the first of the great questions as the Question of Being, he seems to be consciously leaving room for a Catholic interpretation of his words. God has long been defined as 'Being itself', and Heidegger speaks of the impact of the Question of Being upon us as if it can be an overwhelming religious experience. But the Being of which he really speaks is the contingent being that mainstream religious traditions usually describe as trembling on the very brink of crumbling into nothingness. Heidegger really wants us to shiver with religious dread, not before God, but at the thought of all Being's contingency and temporality. And (at least on my interpretation of him) he wants to coax us in the direction of the new religion of life. We'll have to learn to accept and say Yes to, and be really happy with, contingent, finite, temporal be-ing. It's all there is, and religion is going to be the way we learn to dance out over it.

In summary, I have given six examples of the different ways in which various important thinkers and groups have recently seen the great questions of life. They were, respectively, our scientific sages, Kant, the Buddha, Schopenhauer, Nietzsche, and Heidegger. The discussion has illustrated two points: first, there is no agreed standard list of the great questions of life, and second that a particular formulation of the great questions is shaped by the general approach and style of the thinker who is producing it.

I have also suggested that since today philosophy and religious thought are becoming life centred, we should speak of the Great Questions *of Life*. As such they remain popular, despite the fact that many strict philosophers and satirical writers ridicule them. Douglas Adams, in his celebrated *Hitchhiker's Guide to the Galaxy* (1968) mocks the Great Question about Life, the Universe and Everything; but we should not allow him to deter us. He even has the temerity to mock the present writer, who appears in his book in the guise of the theologian Oolon Kolluphid; but we are neither bloodied nor bowed. The fact is that the great questions are still the ordinary person's usual point of entry into the world of religious and philosophical thought. We may distinguish three groups of them. They are:

1. *Questions about the meaning, point, or worth of It All.*

These are the questions that arouse the ire of many philosophers, including Wittgenstein. I want my life to be given a ready-made plot, script, and goal, probably by God, because I am nostalgic for the good old days when people felt that the 'meaning' or the purpose of their lives was predestined and already laid on for them, and I am still reluctant to undertake full moral responsibility for my own life. Wittgenstein rightly disliked the weakness of those who ask: 'What's the meaning of life?' 'What's the *point* of It All?' and 'What makes It All worthwhile?' Even the lowliest insect cares about life enough to struggle for life until it dies: can't we at least do as well as *that*? Look at the wasp on the windowpane, battling for life: is it a braver and better creature than you are?

2. *Speculative questions in metaphysics and cosmology.*

These are venerable issues such as the existence of God and of the immortal human soul, and (today) the nature of mind, consciousness, selfhood, etc. In general, these questions are either already pretty conclusively answered by the way philosophy has developed since Kant, or they are in principle answerable. At least they are not incurably mysterious and unmanageable: on the contrary, one can be pretty confident that one (broadly) knows how to set about answering them.

3. *Questions about Be-ing, or finite being: that is, about coming to be and passing away; about temporality, contingency, and finitude.*

These are the most interesting and serious questions, as Heidegger rightly (more or less) saw. As people say: life is a one-way ticket and there are no retakes. Everything happens only once, and you get only one chance. Everything is utterly irrevocable and final and so infinitely serious, or infinitely insignificant; or (being *both*), it is infinitely comical or absurd. And it's all *that* that fills us with religious feeling for life.

5

GETTING THE HORRORS

The present argument is trying and must keep a number of balls in the air at once, so I need to recapitulate. In Christian and post-Christian societies people are still almost unanimous in equating religious beliefs with beliefs that invoke a higher and more powerful supernatural world. Each individual believer sees herself as the focus of a war between good and evil: every soul is a cosmic battleground, for the supernatural order everywhere impinges upon the everyday world, planning and directing the course of events so as to achieve the fulfilment of its long-term purposes for us. This picture of how things are with us may be described as a picturesque—or as they used to say in Britain, 'tuppence-coloured'[1]—version of Platonism, Christianity's chief historic ally, for while Platonism remained a powerful influence upon people's general world-picture it helped greatly to make Christian theology seem intelligible and even plausible.

To be religious, on this account, then, is to be a person who thinks that to live aright in this world we must refer continually to an invisible higher world that is intensely interested in our performance. One must go via the supernatural world; one needs to consult it and to keep it in mind at all times. It seems in retrospect to have been a strangely paranoiac vision, rather like a conspiracy theory, and Kierkegaard actually compares being a Christian to being a spy—someone who lives by a secret allegiance that other people around him do not know about. On this view of religion faith is always somewhat indirect, and always trades upon the ancient distinction between appearance and reality.

However, during the last few centuries the enormous growth of modern knowledge has changed things utterly. We now live not in a cosmos made long ago by commanding divine words, but in a changing human lifeworld that is generated and held within the conversation of ordinary humanity. As things are now, there are only white noise, the formless, outpouring, prelinguistic flux of Be-ing, and human language that struggles to pattern it and shape it into an agreed-upon habitable world. The world-pictures we come up with have, for the most part, about the same degree of objective truth in them as has a full pictorial representation of the constellations in the night sky. There is no supernatural order: there is only one world, the slowly changing human lifeworld, the world that we continually make and remake.

Religion must now take a new form. It must become immediate, and fully immanent. It has to be about the way we all feel about and relate to life in general, and to our own lives in particular. It is about the principles and values that are to guide our creative, world-building activity.

What are its special problems? There is the constant struggle to establish and maintain a sufficient consensus, but that's not impossible, for we are social animals with a strong interest in coming to agreement with others. More seriously, our preliminary review of the attitudes of some influential modern thinkers to the old topic of the great questions of life has led us to recognize the merits of Heidegger's formulation of the issues.

Let us restate. There is no ready-made real world out there for us. There is only the unending human labour of building and trying to maintain a consensus human lifeworld. The daily labour of modern democratic politics well reflects the situation that human beings are always in—trying to build a common world that will be strong, broad, and elastic enough to give you and me and him and her the space to pursue each of us our own vision of the good life.

What threatens this very reasonable endeavour? We are through-and-through linguistic beings, who build our common world with language and who by language are made highly reflective. We cannot but be aware that life is subject to certain very general limits. Everything comes to be and passes away; all be-ing is temporal; everything is contingent—subject to 'hap', chance, or (if you like) 'happenstance'—and finally, everything is finite, including not only all our powers but also life itself, which ends in death.

In developed Platonism people were encouraged to look to the supernatural world for deliverance from these limitations. Life is merely temporal, but God is eternal; we, all our powers, and our lifespans, are only finite, but God is infinite; with us everything is contingent, but with God everything is necessary; we live in a world of universal coming to be and passing away, but in the heavenly world everything is unchangeably the same forever. Religion was thus presented as a way of *escape* from everything that is wrong with this world and this life. But as Platonism died we lost the hope of ever seeing any radically better world. It began to seem instead that we are permanently stuck with the metaphysical limitations of this life. Religion has to change sharply. Instead of being a way of *escaping* from time, chance, and death, it will have to become *a way of accepting and affirming this life, with all its limits, as a package deal.* An immediate religion of life has got to be stated, and it will be a religion that says yes to transience, yes to happenstance, and yes even to life's end in death, when our work is done and we need to be content to leave the scene so that the next generation can take over. We need a religion that will show us that although we are only transient beings, and although we will never know a setup that differs in any radical way from the present one, it is nevertheless possible for us to commit ourselves to life so completely that we do experience eternal joy in life and can say that it has all been worthwhile. We may have been given a very bad time, or we may have had a bad time, but by solar living we can touch the top; and then we can learn to say: 'I regret nothing, I am not complaining at all, and I don't wish that anything had been different. I am ready simply to say amen, and depart in peace.'

That's the most there can be for us—by which I mean that it is the most we can now expect any religion to be able to deliver. But it's what we should look for and should expect to find.

We will shortly review the great questions of life—or at least we will review a sample of them, including both some formulations that I do not care for and some others that I like. But before we do that I need to consider a fundamental difficulty of a (broadly) Wittgensteinian kind. It is this: the general philosophical position to which we are drawn holds that 'life has no outside'; that is to say, the language-formed human lifeworld is all there is. Nothing outside it can be known or even thought. We must give up the idea that we can somehow step right out of or 'transcend' the human situation, looking at it as if from outside and descrying its most general characteristics. But will we not then be forced to conclude that philosophy is largely a waste of time? We'll do better if we remain immediately absorbed in life. Each morning I sit in my study, ruminating and trying to get down a few words about It All, or about life; but a scatty young person out clubbing, gossiping, and living it up is probably more sensibly occupied than I am. According to my own doctrines I should give up philosophy and *Get a life!* Shouldn't I?

What answer have I to that? I agree that life is outsideless. I can't draw a line all round it and think both sides of the line: I can't totalize life, thinking it as a whole and describing its most general features and laws. But I can do the sort of thing that Hegel and Kierkegaard do when they are exploring different forms of consciousness and ways of life as from within. I can describe life immanently, as from a point inside it. I can take something within life as an art image of life as a whole, in the way that filmmakers do when they present us with the images of a market, a theatre, a busy and brightly lit city-centre street in the late evening, or perhaps commuters piling out of a train, or tramping back and forth across a bridge. Such images are familiar, and they may embolden us to point out that I don't have to transcend life altogether to be able to see it clearly and say something interesting about it. The point about art is that it gives us a kind of understanding that is neither metaphysical nor scientific: it presents us with a powerful compressed image of the whole of which it and we are part, and thereby gives us something like general understanding on the basis of a single case, selected and observed with great accuracy and care. And a modern religious writer can surely attempt to write about life in some such way.

A second line of argument to establish that an (admittedly rather loose-knit and literary) philosophy of life is possible depends upon my 'democratic' method of collecting and interpreting all the new idioms in ordinary language that pithily represent what we currently think and feel about life.[2] This method, so far rather oddly neglected, turns out to be unexpectedly productive and illuminating.

I do not accept, therefore, Wittgenstein's mood of anti-philosophy that sometimes led him to urge his students to give up philosophy and instead just immerse themselves in 'real life'. On the contrary, I am defending an approach to religious thought through the philosophy of life. It begins with our modern 'Empty radical humanism': there is only and outsidelessly the changing human lifeworld, generated by our common struggle to impose public order and significance upon the outpouring flux of chaotically contingent Be-ing (crossed out if you prefer, which by admitting that it's not a proper word fits it to be a sign for non-language). Next we explore the world of 'life' immanently, examining the principal art images of life and the principal idioms in which we currently voice our thoughts and feelings about life.

Then, third, we attempt an appraisal of the great questions of life. What are they, and what sort of accounts of them do people give? So far we have found that there is no generally agreed list of what the great questions are supposed to be. Different thinkers, setting up their personal approaches to philosophy, come up with somewhat different accounts of the great questions. I have indicated that I think that Heidegger is one of the best guides: his account of the questions is evidently related to the old Leibnizian doctrine of 'metaphysical evil'. Because we are finite creatures, we cannot realize all our lives simultaneously, but must take things in and do things bit-by-bit. That means we must live in time, which in turn means that we must be subject to contingency and to mortality. The great questions of life, the daunting, fearsome mysteries that surround our lives, have to do with the way everything comes to be and passes away, and everything is subject to time and chance and death. Including me. And you.

Here an important and interesting difference from our main religious tradition becomes apparent. In Latin Christian theology the big issue that drives the whole story is *sin*— the threat it presents to God's design for the whole of creation, and what God is doing about it. But on my account 'sin' is largely dead. For me religion now starts from the great threat posed to our well-being and happiness by our dread and horror at the endless, shapeless, and almost *oceanic* heaving flux of life, at the relentless, irrevocable passing of time, at the vulnerability of everything and everyone to sheer chance, and at the blankness of death.

Leibniz and his generation did not yet find 'metaphysical evil' to be much of a problem. If the temporality, contingency, and finitude of all things in our world caused us to fret, it was so that they could function as *pointers* to the invisible world, where we can satisfy our souls with things that are eternal, necessary, and infinite. Today there is only the human world, and metaphysical evil is apt to give us the horrors. We're stuck with it.

In this situation, the main job of religion now is to transform our intense feelings of dread, horror, and metaphysical giddiness into blissful religious feeling. The negative feelings here involved are intensely personal: it is the self that feels small, sick, and terrified, and religion's cure involves using their very violence and excess to break them free from the self. This suddenly and startlingly transforms these negative feelings because, contrary to what the Platonists always say, beliefless, 'noncognitive' religion *can* be religion that really does work well, *as religion!*

More of that in due course. Meanwhile, I am proposing that there are four of these very frightening and overwhelming negative emotions to which we are subject. They are, in the first place, the absence from the human world as we now perceive it of any secure anchorage, any objective realities, certainties, fixed points, or guiderails to cling to. On the contrary the human world, which is the world of language, is like the ocean; and when we realize this it can make us feel seasick or nauseous.

Second, there is the irrevocability and only-onceness of time, slipping away and gradually entombing us like Winnie in Beckett's *Happy Days*, as the range of open possibilities before us gets narrower and narrower.

Third, there is our dread at our lives' contingency and our constant statistical vulnerability to misfortune and disaster. Eventually we find ourselves waiting for the blow to fall. It will fall eventually, but we don't know when. So we just wait. This statistical vulnerability to sickness, or mischance, or whatever has come to be widely appreciated only since the seventeenth century, with the decline of belief in divine predestination and the rise of the insurance industry with its tables of mortality and varied ways of assessing risk. But it now plays a prominent part in our thinking: each of us knows that his world, or her world, may suddenly collapse without any warning, and must live with that knowledge.

Finally there is our fear of death, which has not been lessened by the great increase in our expectation of life. Everything is finite: nothing lasts forever—not even our life.

I emphasize that these four negative emotions—the feelings of radical insecurity, of gradual entombment, of the eventual running out of our luck, and of horror and dread as death approaches—all get their peculiar fearsomeness from the way in which they fasten upon the quaking self. We urgently need a cure for them, and the cure involves breaking them free from the self. Running free and non-fixated, the emotions involved are surprisingly easily transformed by religion to become cosmic and blissful.

6

RELIGIOUS FEELING, HEALTHY AND SICK

On January 30, 2004, at Kassel, Germany, a forty two-year old man named Armin Meiwes was convicted of manslaughter. Meiwes is reported to have been a socially isolated and lonely man who felt unable to form close relationships. He seems to have conceived the idea that he could enter into really intimate communion with another person only if he could find someone willing to be killed and eaten by him. He advertised his desire on the Internet, and soon had around two hundred volunteers. The rest of the story has been publicized all over the world.

Books about the case will doubtless follow in due course, and Meiwes' psychology and his precise language will be closely examined. We can be sure that the influence of Christian thought and practice upon the whole story will be pointed out. It is especially apparent in the eroticization of physical suffering and death, and in the attempt to achieve an intense and intimate communion with the victim by 'eating his flesh and drinking his blood', an idea that is already presented in surprisingly—even shockingly—literal terms in St John's Gospel (6:52–58).[1] Still within the very earliest Christian period, the eroticization of the desire for suffering and martyrdom first appears in the (probably second-century) writer St Ignatius of Antioch. From these beginnings a straight line of development runs to the treatment of the passion and death of Christ and his saints in Baroque art, in which expressions of Christian piety have become barely distinguishable from sadomasochistic pornography.

It should not be supposed that Christian art is unique in allowing piety to run surprisingly close to pornography. A well-known wall painting at Pompeii depicting flagellation leaves the spectator unsure whether it is to be read religiously or erotically, and historians of religion will surely comment that such ambiguity is not at all unusual.

All this creates a problem for me. I want to give a noncognitive and naturalistic account of religion. That will require me to give an account of the emotional dynamics of religion, and in particular of the way religion can transform negative and painful feelings of horror, sick terror, and nausea at the human condition into rapturous, cosmic feelings of bliss and joyful acceptance. If my whole life is being poisoned by anxiety and horror at the radical insecurity of our existence and the prospect of physical and mental decline and death that faces us all, then surely I should welcome and gratefully seize the chance of being cured of these fears by religion? And my problem is that I am not sure how to draw a clear line between those cultural-religious transformations of natural feeling that are benign and valuable, and those that are sinister and sexually perverse. It is a well-known fact that our psychology tends to make the unbearable bearable by eroticizing it: but what are the limits?

In *The Way to Happiness*, I quoted what seems to be a familiar and clearly benign case of transformation, namely the case where the feelings of vertigo that normally attack us on a cliff-top, or a mountaintop, or when we lean forward out of a high-rise building, are transformed by culture into highly pleasurable feelings of religious awe and aesthetic delight before 'the sublime' in nature.

I usually have no serious doubt about the goodness of the transformed feeling in such a case. I am always very ready, when a few fine days are in prospect, to drive about two hundred miles and spend a fair amount of money just to have the chance to walk up somewhere like Wild Boar Fell, sit on the Nab, and gaze at the view I love so much. The feelings of exaltation, peace, and acceptance that I associate with a number of such places are intense, so intense that I am prepared to take a good deal of trouble to indulge them.

However, there are similar cases that are less benign. A long coastal path, which at many points runs along the flanks of steep slopes and cliffs, winds around the southwest 'toe' of England, going west along Somerset, Devon, and Cornwall and then back eastwards along the Channel coast to Dorset. The landscape along this great path is often exceedingly beautiful: but I have on two occasions walked it when I felt psychologically troubled, and felt so overwhelming a surge of desire to commit suicide just by misplacing a foot and toppling over sideways that I had to leave the path hastily and move inland. The two landscapes in question were a mile or two west of Linton, and east of Lulworth, and so beautiful in high summer that I wanted to die into them, like the proverbial person who sees Naples and is ready to die. I am talking about a strong impulse to suicide. One is aware that religious experience may have the effect of delivering one suddenly from anxiety and the fear of death—but one doesn't want death to become quite *that* attractive. Not just yet.

I think the point I am making here is that religion—and culture generally—obviously do have great power to displace, redirect, and otherwise transform our feelings. But it is a slippery, ambiguous, and sometimes even dangerous business—as when we are shocked to discover that highly pleasurable feelings of awe and delight before great natural beauty may run alarmingly close to an intense yearning for immediate death. In Latin Christianity, the cult of the martyrs and the practice of dwelling with loving devotion upon the physical sufferings of Jesus can notoriously 'groom' people for psychological perversion—by which I mean not just 'S and M', but serious, physically dangerous sadomasochism.

How do we learn to draw the lines in these matters? The answer is surely that both religion and culture generally do take a great deal of trouble to set ritual boundaries. For example, I mentioned earlier the ontological insecurity, the seasickness and even the nausea we may feel if we are sensitive to the contingency of everything, and the lack of firm objective reality, truth, and value in our postmodern world-picture. How can we live and be happy once we have really understood the fragility of our truths, our values—even of our existence itself? How can we get into the habit of dancing out over sheer contingency and trusting it to support us? It seems that what we do (especially when we are young) is learn to strengthen our own nerve by deliberately courting danger. We take up hazardous sports, recreations, and occupations. We test ourselves and especially our ability to look death in the eye and keep our nerve. Whether it's rock climbing, soldiering, or motorcycle racing, we are taught to keep cool, avoid unnecessary risks, and follow standard procedures. With practice and disciplined following of the rule book, one can learn to live with a high degree of insecurity.

In religion, rather similar conclusions had been reached by late antiquity. It is not easy to know what is rational religious practice. On the whole, one should not court martyrdom, one should avoid excessive asceticism, and one should avoid public displays of individual zeal. One can learn more and do better simply by submitting oneself to the discipline of following a communal rule of life.

How do we draw the line in the case we have discussed, that of rapture or thoughts of suicide? In the latter case, what went wrong: what line was crossed? I think the difference is this: religion is normally cosmic emotion, that is, strong overflowing feeling that has become freed from its usual biological roots in the needs of the self. But in the pathological case the feeling wasn't *freed from* the self: it was *turned back against* the self, so that I passionately desired to find liberation through self-destruction. This suggests to me that we should be wary of traditional religious talk about putting the self to death, or mortifying it, as a way to happiness. Such talk can become too attractive. It also suggests to me that Schopenhauer's way to salvation, by turning the will to live in oneself against itself, sounds like the desire for suicide, and is objectionable. In religion it is right to seek a blissful freedom from self-concern, but self-hatred is never a good thing.

7

SHORT ANSWERS TO THE GREAT QUESTIONS

Because there are no standard formulations of the great questions, or even any agreement about what they are, this present review cannot pretend to be complete. But in one way or another my list of questions includes most of what I have mentioned so far, and all the others I can think of. (Six supplementary questions are held back for later chapters.) I begin with some typical formulations of the most common and most general question of all.

> *Why are we here?*
> *Why were we put on this earth?*
> *What are we here for?*

1

This is a thoroughly misleading and irritating question—rather like the proverbial one: *Have you stopped beating your wife yet? Answer me: Yes or No!* The latter question both assumes and tries to hide the assumption that you *are* presently beating your wife. It demands a straight answer, but the question isn't straight itself. Similarly, *Why are we here?* assumes there must be some reason why we are here: it assumes we are justified in expecting an answer that will relate the whole of human existence in all its variety to the fulfilment of a single great cosmic moral purpose, by which and for which we were (presumably) specially created, and then 'put on this earth'. But we have no evidence for the belief that everything in human life everywhere can be related to the fulfilment of one great cosmic plan. On the contrary:

A. The greatest and most important quantum leap forward in the entire history of human knowledge occurred when, around the time of Galileo and Descartes, we consciously abandoned teleological explanation (explanation in terms of purposes) and instead invented critical thinking and modern science. In a word, we have found that how-questions can be asked and answered profitably, but the why-question is a complete waste of time. Forget the why-question. Just by asking it we have already made a bad mistake: we are demanding back the very thing that we earlier ruled out, namely, ready-made and built-in purposiveness. It isn't there. Of course it isn't. You *know* it isn't.

B. The huge variety and excessiveness of the human lifeworld recalls the variety and excessiveness of biological life—for example, on a coral reef or in a rainforest. It is much too vast and varied, and too often at odds with itself, to be explained as being all of it the product of a single great mind bent upon executing a single cosmic moral purpose. But evolutionary theory has shown convincingly and in great detail how all this stupendous variety can have arisen as the product simply of chance and time, mutations and natural selection. Evolution explains excess much better than monotheism can. Life always battles to try out every possibility and to fill all the available slots. Life seeks to maximize itself, not for any moral reason, but just for its own sake: that's life.

These two arguments are I think sufficient by themselves to warn us off any ideas of an extra-human purposiveness pervading the world, connecting all events, and ultimately certain to bring everything to a single glorious consummation. Admittedly, such ideas have been tenacious: the liberal belief in progress and 'the perfectibility of Man' lasted until the 1970s, and communism until 1990 or so. The 'dream' of the building of the kingdom of God on earth is still occasionally referred to, as in Martin Luther King Jr.'s Washington speech of the 1960s and John Lennon's song *Imagine* of the 1970s. But the most basic presumptions of science are not at all likely to shift: we must give up the idea of an objective, universal purposiveness that guides events and morally unifies the world. The only world there is, is *our* world, and the only purposes we will ever detect at work in the world are our own.

2   *What is the meaning of life?*
     What is the point of it all?
     What's it all about?

The first group of questions related especially to the desire of human beings to find a single cosmic moral purpose into which we can each of us fit the story of our own life. This second group of questions sees the world as a whole as presenting us with some kind of riddle. Maybe by hard thinking we can work out the solution, or perhaps there is some privileged person or some religion that has the right answer.

On this view the world is a puzzle—even a sort of crossword puzzle. It is full of signs and clues: it needs to be read carefully. Such an account of the world has often been popular in periods where mathematical physics is not yet dominant, and it is common in the scriptures of various faiths, in the sixteenth century, and in certain postmodern quarters today. It has its attractions: the world is indeed covered all over with language and symbolism, and much of it reflects or bears upon the way things are with us. But we need to remember that we, and we alone, invented language, and we projected onto nature all the ideas, the order, and the feelings that we see in her. So it is scarcely surprising that every little breeze seems to whisper *Louise!* for we are hearing our own voices, echoing back to us. *We* made the world, our poets and our physicists, our weather forecasters, and our mapmakers. We did it to familiarize or domesticate our environment, adapting it to ourselves, naming things and describing them in terms of what they can mean to us.

All of this shows that we don't have and can't have the slightest reason to suppose that the world has *a prehuman, built-in, ready-made meaning of its own* that might mean something to us, in addition to all the patterns and meanings that we have projected onto it. The idea is absurd. If you doubt this, try to say what it would be like for one of the constellations in the night sky to be, not just a projected human picture, but *really* out there. For that matter, what would it be for a law of nature to be really out there? Laws of nature are never *discovered*: they are always *invented*, by us.

Does it matter?
What's the point?
Does anything matter?
What does it all matter?
In the long run we are all dead. (J. M. Keynes)
If Darwin's right, we are just accidental by-products
of a meaningless universe, and nothing
we do makes any real difference.
(Evangelical apologetics)

3

In the old, cosy religious cosmologies that were dominant around the world until the end of the Middle Ages, everybody had a hot line to the heart of things. The cosmic battle between good and evil powers was being fought in—among other places—your own soul. You felt that your choices mattered: indeed, they could scarcely have mattered more.

Science has introduced a new value-free cosmology that dwarfs human beings and is totally alien to us. We'll be very thrilled if one day we discover another tiny corner of the universe that we can inhabit. It is not surprising that at least since Blaise Pascal we've felt that in the modern universe we seem to be utterly insignificant and unimportant.

That is why under this general heading I am gathering together all those formulations of questions about life that in one way or another are asking how, in the face of nature's colossal scale, value-neutrality, and total indifference, can we maintain our confidence that our values matter, our religion matters, even that our *life* matters at all?

This very common feeling shows that we are still nostalgic for the old religious cosmologies, which certainly did supply us with oodles of ready-made meaning, values, and destiny. But we are badly mistaken in being so nostalgic, because we are never again going to have everything laid on for us in the old way. Instead, we've got to get used to the new situation in which we recognise that *we* create everything. *We* make all the meanings, *we* posit all the values, *we* invent religion. It's all up to us. There's no reason why your religion and your values shouldn't mean as much to you in future as ever they meant in the past, provided that you face up honestly to the one truth that religious organizations refuse to face, which is that we now know that it is all up to us. Meaning and truth and value, creed and destiny, are *never again* going to be laid on for us in quite the old way. In future, they are going to be guiding pictures that help some people to live, and they are just as strong as our own loyalty to them: it's up to us.

* * * * *

So far, we have dealt with the questions that in chapter 4 (See p. 44) were labelled 'Questions about the meaning, point, or worth of It All'. In the light of the answers we have given, we can now move on to the second group: '2. Speculative questions in metaphysics and cosmology'.

4 | *Is there a God?*
Does God exist?

This is the only one of the big questions to which I am not able to give a short, straight answer. There are just too many complications, partly over the meaning of 'God' and partly over the idea of 'reality'.

The word 'God' is used in referring both to the one infinite God of metaphysical monotheism and to one or another of a very, very different class of beings, the finite and intra-cosmic divinities of Indo-European polytheism, the Bible's 'gods many and lords many'. The query *Is there a God?* is so worded as to make one pause and wonder which kind of god the questioner has in mind.

Today, because of the decay of metaphysics, the ordinary believer's God is an imaginary Father—a *finite* being, in time—to whom one listens and with whom one talks. At the same time the ordinary believer invokes the God of non-realism, as when he or she says: 'My God is not a God of Judgement. My God is a God of mercy, forgiveness, and love. Not a God of the respectable only, but also a God who takes the side of the outcast, etc.' In such talk (of which we hear a great deal) God functions as a personification of our most cherished values. So the God of the ordinary believer and the ordinary church leader clearly does not 'literally' exist. The Father in one's head is certainly finite, and seemingly an imaginary being; while the moral personification is evidently ideal rather than actual, because the believer is openly admitting that 'I posit a god whose job is to reflect my own cherished values, and in whom I can therefore believe'. Today's popular religion is therefore non-realist and will be quite happy to remain so—but with one qualification: it oddly insists upon its own realistic character, even though it is totally unable to spell out exactly what God's 'objective reality' is.

At this point there is another level of complication. Plato's doctrine of a 'noumenal' or intelligible world of Ideas provided the basic vocabulary for describing the way the superior reality of God and the heavenly world differs from the everyday reality of empirical things here below in the visible world. The difference can be expressed in an analogy: the eternal reality of God is to empirical, sensible reality as *a priori* truth—i.e., truth in mathematics and formal logic—is to empirical or factual truth. Hearing this, I say at once: 'Ah, yes. That means that God's reality is abstract, universal, conventional, axiomatic, like maths. So God isn't a bit like an actual being. God is a universal abstract spiritual ideal'. But others say: 'Certainly not! Plato was a realist. For him, the "reality" of noumenal things was certainly *not* merely ideal and abstract—they were much greater, and *more* real, than sensible things. That's why in Christian Platonism God is *ens realissimum*, the most real thing of all'.

The disagreement I have just described is very sharp and has persisted for many centuries. It's a disagreement about kinds of reality, and there's no sign of it going away just yet. But I can now give as short and straight an answer as is possible to the question 'Is there a God?' It is as follows:

the actual, finite God—the ordinary believer's imaginary Father—does not exist. The God of the old Platonic metaphysics, the most-real Being, infinite and unchangeable, has failed too: there is general agreement that he cannot be proved to exist, but ordinary believers have in any case never been able to cope with the infinite, timeless, and impassible God of the old theistic orthodoxy. They want anthropomorphism and always will: they want interaction with their god. Ordinary believers want only a finite God, and want their god to be real.

The non-realist God, who is a guiding spiritual ideal and an embodiment of our religious values, could continue to play a part in the religious life—provided only that we are willing to be honest about the status of such a god. But we are not, for the ordinary believer also insists upon a realist understanding of her language about the personal God, even though she cannot spell it out clearly. The muddle has become so bad that I now think it probably best to follow the Buddhists and try to show that it is possible to live a full and fruitful religious life without mentioning God.

In answer to the question, 'Is there a God?' I reply that for the present we'd do better to give up using the word. It's surrounded by too much muddle and dishonesty, and its use at present is doing more harm than good.

5 Is death the end?

In a word, yes. The young Wittgenstein, writing as a soldier in the First World War, already makes most of the main points.[1] The world and life are one. Our language builds only one world, the human lifeworld, and the human lifeworld has no outside. We are always in life. Life is bounded by death, but we never actually cross the boundary and know that we have crossed it: on the contrary, we do not experience death. We don't go through it. We experience and we mourn the deaths of other people, but there's no need at all ourselves to 'prepare for death', because it is not a state in which we will ever find ourselves. That's why 'death is nothing to us' (Lucretius), and why Spinoza says that 'the free man's wisdom is a meditation not of death, but of life'.[2] The most rational attitude toward death is simply to be utterly committed to life and to love it until one's last breath.

Try to name any major philosopher in the entire Western tradition who has had something genuinely interesting and plausible to say about life after death. Plato's *Phaedo* is a shockingly feeble and unconvincing effort from so great a figure. But who else has done any better? Indeed, who else has done anything?

It is puzzling that people have clung to belief in life after death for so long. Perhaps, like the equally irrational belief in reincarnation, it draws some sustenance from our thoughts about the continuity of culture, about living on in our descendants, and about being remembered by posterity.

How did everything begin?
How did life begin?
What are we? Who made us?
How did consciousness begin?

Since the late eighteenth century these questions have increasingly been taken over by science, and we cannot do better than consult the current scientific stories. In the case of the question about the nature and the first beginnings of subjective consciousness, the participants in the debate still have some philosophical sorting out and clarifying of the issues to do, in order to get themselves in a position to set out clear theories of origin. But I think it probably can be done, and in due course will be done.

Questions about ultimate origins are no longer questions to be dealt with in creation myths. They are scientific questions. But it is essential not to allow the new scientific theories to set themselves up as being a full and adequate replacement for the old religious stories. On the contrary, the new scientific story only does about half as much as we would like it to do. It is projected back from within the network of current theory, and points simply to an ideal limit or *terminus a quo* of current theory.

The point being made here can be illustrated very neatly with reference to 'Big Bang' cosmology. From present-day measurements of the rate at which the universe is expanding it is easy to project back to a time when the universe was a mere point, the initial singularity. But the back-projection is done from *within* current theory: it does not enable us to jump clear of the infant universe and take up an independent standpoint from which we can observe the universe's first coming, or being brought, into being.

We should note then that when one of the great questions gets taken over by science it becomes demystified. The story science tells refuses to give us the old absolute reassurance that we used to get from religion, and that many of us still crave for in our hearts.

Today those of us who remain intensely religious have the special task of learning to renounce the old yearning for absolutes, ultimate explanations, and religious certainties.

7   *Why is it that anything at all exists: why is there not just nothing?*

From the time of Leibniz and his formulation of the principle of sufficient reason, theistic apologists have often argued that the ultimate mystery is the bare fact that anything at all exists. There being nothing at all would not be odd, and wouldn't call for any special explanation. But the principle of sufficient reason assures us that for any existing fact or state of affairs whatsoever there is always a sufficient reason why it is so, and not otherwise. Such sufficient reasons may take the form of causes, or choices. But a cause is not an ultimately sufficient reason, for it opens up a regress of causes. To close the regress, the search for an ultimate explanation must always terminate in a great founding choice, a choice of the best made by a being unlimited in wisdom, power and goodness. Therefore God exists.

Thus Leibniz's argument when fully developed aims to show that if any finite things and states of affairs actually exist, then the only ultimate and completely satisfying explanation of them will show them as having been created by a god who is perfect in power, wisdom, and goodness. *En passant*, Leibniz has even solved the problem of evil, for he has demonstrated that this is and must be the best of all possible worlds. For, to be fully explicable, the world must have been the best option available at the moment of the great founding choice that created it. But it is, and so it was.

By this argument, Leibniz has notoriously exposed himself to ridicule, and invites us to question his dogmatic rationalism. The principle of sufficient reason assures us that we are fully entitled to assume there is always a reason for everything: the nature of things is already and at every point geared up to deliver to us in full exactly the sort of ultimate and absolute reassurance and satisfaction that the dogmatist yearns for. In Leibniz's universe there is no contingency: all relations are internal, all truths are analytic, and everything just unfolds its own preexistent nature. In the end, it's a rather boring and deterministic vision. I prefer to point out that Leibniz does not really prove the principle of sufficient reason. Wouldn't he have to assume it to prove it? As it is, however, everything is contingent; everything that is just *happens* to be. The questions, 'Why does anything exist? Why is there not just nothing?' only get raised, of course, in a situation where there *is* something—for example, the questioner. Where there is nothing and no one, the question is not heard; that's all.

* * * * *

By emphasizing the loose-knit, temporal, and contingent character of everything, the discussion so far has prepared us for the third and last group of great questions, those referred to in chapter 4 (See p. 45), above: '3. Questions about Be-ing; that is, about coming to be and passing away: about temporality, contingency, and finitude'. I indicated earlier the spirit in which we approach the core questions that remain. The human lifeworld, the world of Empty radical humanism, is a demystified world. There is only the purely contingent forthcoming of Be-ing, which is nothing but bare possibility, waiting to be fixed or closed by language; and there is the flow of language, trying to fix and hold steady a tolerably clear picture of the world and of ourselves. That's all. And in this world of ordinary life, fluid and without fixed points as it is, I am all the time oscillating between tragedy and comedy, between thinking that my life is infinitely serious and thinking that my life is utterly absurd. This value-instability is uncomfortable, but it is an instability that religion recognizes and can help us to cope with.

That's our situation now. What are the great questions that it raises? As I have indicated, they are about time, contingency, and finitude. Although I am now at an age at which one feels fairly sure of one's opinions about a wide range of questions, I still find *time* very mysterious and hard to think about. And I also find loose-knit universal *contingency* and the *finitude* of our lives and all our powers difficult to get clear about. We will discuss these topics through some of the most frequently raised great questions about them.

Is the past real?
Où sont les neiges d'antan? / Where are the snows of yesteryear? 8

The customary division of tenses in modern Western languages into past, present, and future prompts most of us occasionally to think that perhaps only the present is real. Ahead of the present moment, the future is all the time coming into the narrow bandwidth of material that is presently in motion in my central nervous system and my sense organs. But this bandwidth seems to be a kind of knife-edge, because within a fraction of a second my sense-experiences and thoughts are already fading away into memory. We are likely to think of the cinematic analogy, which seems to suggest that the present moment is only about one-tenth of a second wide.

How is it, then, that the world doesn't look flickery, but on the contrary appears rather stable? It seems that although our eyes are darting about all the time, our brains are busily at work filling in the background and stablilizing the world.

I look out of the window over Parker's Piece, Cambridge. Within 0.1 seconds my eyes flicker over about one-fiftieth of the whole field of view. The rest is hazy but stable, filled in by the brain. And that is my world. Mostly a construct, and only about 0.1 seconds thick. The past does not really exist. Traces of it survive in our memories, and in journals, letters, and other written materials, but for huge tracts of the past we can find neither memories nor written records, and must presumably conclude that it is gone absolutely. Dying people have often hinted to me of their fear that within a few decades or generations they will be totally forgotten.

Such absolute oblivion is disagreeable to contemplate, and we may remember here that our talk about time is often befuddled by an excess of rather misleading and often conflicting metaphors. Perhaps if we change the picture, we will get a different result?

I suggest that we drop the classification of times into past, present, and future, and instead adopt the simple and clear classification used in Classical Hebrew, which draws a distinction between what is already finished (the perfect tense) and what is in readiness and will soon come upon us (the imperfect tense). On this elemental and beautiful view (which I here somewhat oversimplify) there are only two tenses: what's already done, and what is still pending, in process of being settled. Next we translate all this into modern terms, distinguishing between everything that the human conversation has accumulated up to now, the whole of what may be called the modern world, or modern knowledge and, on the other hand, what we still have to do by way of further modifying or elaborating our world, and ourselves.

On this new view, we have divided the whole world into just two zones. The perfect tense embraces the whole of the past and the left-hand side of the present; and the imperfect tends embraces the right-hand side of the present moment, and the future. The past has now become 'real': it is the entire present accumulation of the world, as we have together built it up to now. It is relatively closed and settled. As for the future, it is open; it is what we are working on, what we have in hand, what is still to be determined, what is yet to come.

This change in the way we think of time has some rather cheerful consequences. The past is real: it is the whole world that is before me. And the dead are still with me. I look through their eyes, and see *their* world as one constituent of my world.

> *What does it all mean?*
> *It doesn't mean anything in particular, it just happens.*
> *What am I meant to be doing / cut out for?*
> *If it has got your number on it, that's it.*
> *That's it.*

9

Somewhat to my surprise, I don't find any clearly formulated great question that crystallizes the mystery of contingency. Rather, I find running through our whole tradition an unresolved debate between two strands of thinking.

Those who believe in providence and predestination, together with certain rationalists like Leibniz, insist that we ought to be able to regard everything and accept everything as *meant*—foreordained and therefore in effect necessitated. A great cosmic purpose runs everywhere: it is there to be consulted, to be bowed to, to be collaborated with, to be accepted. Everything that is so, is *meant* to be as it is. Amen.

On the other hand, an equally strong tradition of thought insists that everything is contingent, a matter of hap. It *turns out*, it *befalls*. Consider for example a whole group of words that echo the falling of a die: incident, accident, coincidence, etc., all related to Latin *cadere*, to fall. On this view, whatever happens just happens to happen the way it does, and might have happened otherwise. When we are thinking about whether you will happen to catch a particular disease, we seem quite clearly to regard much happening as a matter of statistical probability, a matter of chance or luck; and it is very noticeable that even in the main Western tradition of Augustinian thought, which is officially predestinarian, there is at the same time much talk of 'the changes and chances of this mortal life' and of 'the frailty of our mortal nature'.

Do we or do we not regard pure contingency as being frightening and 'meaningless'? I am unsure: sometimes, as I have noted elsewhere, we are greatly attracted to luck, fortune, and games of chance. It is also worth noting that our language supplies the notion of 'your number' as being intermediate between divine predestination and pure chance. During the Second World War civilians went to bed each night knowing that they might suddenly die as the result of a direct hit in a bombing raid. They didn't like the thought that it was all a matter of pure uncontrolled chance, nor did there seem to be any great comfort in the thought that they'd only be hit if it was God's will that they should take a hit. So they resorted to an intermediate position by shrugging their shoulders and saying: 'Well, if the bomb's got my number on it . . .'. Perhaps this was a sort of fatalism. One also heard at that time: 'One day my number will come up'. Perhaps this implied that 'life is a lottery'.

Yet so unresolved are our feelings about all this that an equally strong tradition in our language prefers to see lotteries and chance as benign! The Old Norse word for luck or chance, *hap*, gives us not only happening but also 'happiness'; and the Latin word that is exactly equivalent to hap, *fors*, meaning luck or chance, gives us not only fortuitous but also 'fortune' and 'fortunate'.

I have to conclude that this is another of those areas in our language where we choose to keep two conflicting lines of thought going because we do not care to come down decisively either one way or the other.

* * * * *

With that we complete the present review of (most of) the great questions of life, noting that they have turned out to fall into three groups.

The largest group, including 1–5 and 7, turn out upon examination to express an irrepressibly strong yearning and nostalgia for the comfort and security—the sense of being *at home*—that was provided by the old religious cosmologies that we have recently lost. People still wish they could believe in an objective, founding, and guaranteeing reason out there, a meaning and purpose out there, values out there, ultimate security and protection out there. They don't like the thought of being 'alone and afraid / In a world I never made'. They don't like the new 'Empty radical humanism', and they are irresistibly drawn to the old realism. I guess most of them think that the ultimate question behind all the great questions is that of the objective existence and the goodness of God.

The second group of great questions that we have found are the cluster of questions about how things first began, which have now been taken over by science—and are therefore no longer really great questions at all. No. 6 summarized them.

Finally, the third group of great questions are ones that seem to arise around the margins of the modern worldview. *How is it that everything is temporal in the way it is? How is it that everything is contingent in the way it is?* and *How is it that everything is finite in the way it is?* My suspicion about this third group of great questions is that we are not yet managing to frame them clearly because we are still in process of assimilating the new worldview. When we see more clearly where we now are, I guess that the central mystery will have to do with understanding outsidelessness and accepting its implications.

8

THE QUESTION OF 'ULTIMATE REALITY'

We have not yet considered another great question that pops up quite frequently in ordinary language, namely the question of 'ultimate reality'.

> *What is ultimately real?*
> *What is the nature of ultimate reality?*   **10**

This is not a simple question to answer. We begin with the word 'real', pointing out that the chief interest of ordinary language is never in metaphysics, but always in ethics and the business of living. In ordinary language the real is rather like the true: the real is what you can rely upon, and what you must reckon with. When people are becoming rather fanciful, we recall them to the real:

> Get real!
> In sober reality
> The reality is that . . .
> You must face reality
> You are losing touch with reality

In philosophy what is real is usually taken to be what exists out there, objectively, and independent both of our minds and of our language. In that case the supremely real or ultimately real is naturally described as existing *a se* (of itself), as self-existent Being, or as the absolute.

Ordinary language's vocabulary is rather different. If the real is the reliable, the most real will be described as a rock, the rock of ages, a mighty fortress, something in which or by clinging to which one can find personal security. The mark of the real, in philosophy, is that *it* doesn't need *me*; but, in religion, is *my* desperate need of *it*.

Thus the quest for the real leads philosophy towards the impassible God of dogmatic realist metaphysics, and ordinary people to the God of personal faith, the Rock. But where do you look, and how do you look? Ordinary language is very familiar with the classical philosophical contrast between appearance and reality, and rings a surprisingly large number of changes upon it:

> appearance / reality
> outward / inward
> surface / depth
> manifest / latent
> exterior / interior
> first impressions / second thoughts
> foundation or base / superstructure

And so on. In ordinary language the phrase most commonly used to draw attention to these contrasts is '… only the tip of the iceberg', a phrase that is used to warn us that what's really there, underneath, may be very much bigger than what appears on the surface, or may be markedly different from what appears on the surface. In religious language the contrast is a serious matter. For example, God remarks *à propos* Jesse's son Eliab that 'man looks on the outward appearance, but the LORD looks on the heart'[1]—the heart in religious language being equivalent to inner reality in ordinary language.

On other occasions, we make jokes about the appearance/reality distinction. People like to quote the swan which appears above the surface to be gliding smoothly over the water, but underneath may be having to paddle furiously. And everyone has heard of the girl who criticizes a pretentious young man of her acquaintance by saying of him that, 'He seems deep on the surface, but deep down he's shallow'. Evidently a sharp contrast between outer appearance and inner reality can be comical, or absurd.

To resume the argument, if ordinary language rings many changes on the appearance/ reality distinction, and in many areas of life urges us not to be content to trust our first impressions but to seek the real behind the merely apparent, it would seem that we are being strongly encouraged (a) to develop a theory of degrees of reality, and (b) to seek what is 'ultimately real' behind and beyond all the appearances of life. The ultimately real sounds like God, and this area of ordinary language seems to incorporate one of the most important surviving fragments of the old Christian-Platonist metaphysics.

More than that, we have here a relic of one of the ancient ways to God. The argument again comes ultimately from Plato and is linked with an hierarchical conception of reality. Wherever we make the move from the superficial to the deep, from outward appearance to inner reality, we are moving one rung higher up the ladder of degrees of reality. The highest, at the very top of the ladder, is by definition God. God is the ultimate reality, the Supreme Being, the Most-Real Being.

Now for some complications. Is God then simply the Highest Being, the top rung of the ladder? If so, then God is finite and differs only in degree, and not in kind, from all the lower rungs of the ladder. That can't be right, so perhaps we'd better correct ourselves, and say that the ladder points out and away to an infinite God rather as a shipway points out to the open sea. But in this latter case there is an infinite gulf between even the top rung of the ladder and God, so that—strictly speaking—the ladder hasn't brought us any 'nearer' to God at all. The ontological gulf between the top rung of the ladder and God is still exactly as wide as the ontological gulf between the bottom rung of the ladder and God. In each case, the gulf is infinite.

This difficulty is fatal to many of the traditional proofs of the existence of God—including those put forward by St Thomas Aquinas.[2] Each of Thomas' Five Ways begins by singling out a relation that may be found between two things in the world—a relation such as 'is moved by', or 'is caused by', or 'is less real than'—and then develops the idea of a chain of such relations that leads up to God. In terms of Thomas' own worldview, the hockey ball is hit by the hockey stick, which is swung by the player, whose body is moved by 'the elements', which are moved by the heavenly bodies, which are moved by God. The argument can only work if the relation 'is moved by' passes unaltered from link to link along the chain, all the way to God. But it doesn't: the way in which the infinite God moves the sun and the stars is radically different from the way the hockey stick moves the hockey ball. The move that jumps clear of the world altogether to find the world's Creator is obviously quite different from the move from one thing to another according to a rule, within the world. In which case the so-called Ways do not in fact lead us any 'closer' to God at all.

Once this difficulty was clearly understood you couldn't assume any-more that there must *be* a Highest Being, and that the Highest Being must be God. The whole question of ultimate reality, whatever it is, had to be phrased more cautiously. And that is why in ordinary language today we still occasionally hear the two formulations from which I began:

What is ultimately real?
What is the nature of ultimate reality?

The change took place between Kant and Schopenhauer—that is, in about the year 1800. Kant was the last great thinker who still worked within Plato's deep assumptions and vocabulary, even as he was bringing that tradition to an end. Then, only a few years later, Schopenhauer is very different, because for him (and for Schelling) it was no longer obvious that ultimate reality, when found, must turn out to be One, rational and supremely great or perfect. When he asked himself 'What is the nature of ultimate reality?' Schopenhauer replied: 'It reflects what I find, deep down, in myself and in all life. It is endlessly and incurably restless, unhappy and at odds with itself.'

After Schopenhauer, then, Victorian and modern atheism and pessimism self-consciously broke with the assumption, as old as Parmenides, that ultimate reality must be One, rational and perfect. Instead, modern pessimism follows Thomas Hardy, and takes a tragic view of life. It's unhappy, it's at odds with itself, and so are we.

Against this background it became in due course possible for some people to start wondering about a return to belief in God. These people started from the common presumption of their contemporaries that 'ultimate reality' is coldly indifferent to humans, or that ultimate reality is unhappy and at odds with itself, and then they tried nevertheless to argue that we have been given grounds for believing that 'ultimate reality is gracious', after all. The celebrated Anglican apologist Bishop John A.T. Robinson made a move of this type in his little book *Honest to God* (1963)—but was completely misunderstood by his contemporaries.

It is evident that ordinary people's talk about ultimate reality is not by any means as vague and vapid as it seemed at first. On the contrary, it has a whole complex history behind it. In favour of the expression, it can be said that 'ultimate reality' is a decently neutral way of referring to the slot in the whole scheme of things that was traditionally occupied by God. When we ask, 'What is ultimately real?' we are asking in an open way what is to be put in that slot. And when we ask, 'What is the nature of ultimate reality?' we are asking concerning whatever may turn out to occupy the slot whether it, or he, is, for example, loving and gracious to us humans, or totally indifferent, or a blind, tragic striving, or whatever.

We now return to the title of this chapter, the question of ultimate reality considered as one of the great questions of life. As we have seen, people usually raise the question of ultimate reality by way of trying to reopen the question of metaphysics, the very first move that it calls upon us to make being the move that launches the appearance/reality distinction. The real that we seek is not immediately given to us. To reach the ultimately real we must first undermine confidence in the human lifeworld. It is, we feel, no more than mere sensuous appearance, superficially pleasing but too unstable and mutable to give us any lasting happiness. We must learn to pass through this world of changing appearances and begin training ourselves to think, and indeed to inhabit, the more real, intelligible world beyond—the world of theory, the world of pure forms and timeless truths and values. As we become gradually more proficient in abstract thought, our conception of the intelligible world becomes gradually more uni-fied, until at last the quest for the supremely real culminates in a state of visionary contemplation of an object that is One, eternal, supremely self-intelligible, and timelessly perfect. And *that* is what 'ultimate reality' is.

It will be obvious that I reject outright this whole train of argument, starting with the appearance/reality distinction. After Darwin we were certain eventually to recognize that there is for us only one world, this world, the human lifeworld, that is, the world of our communicative and historical life, the world our language gives us. Any move to downgrade our world to the status of 'mere appearance', and to urge us to seek a 'more real' world elsewhere, is not the first step towards salvation. It is the fall: it alienates us from the only world and the only life we'll ever have.

Our language is a continuum, and our world is a continuum. There is no sense in trying to split it between, for example, mental and material realms. Look at a modern novel, and see how seamlessly its language runs across both the realm of physical objects and the realm of subjective feel-ing and experience. The alleged 'problem of consciousness' doesn't trouble the novel one bit.[3] It is, in fact, a pseudo-problem.

Our world is one, and a continuum; but more than that, we continually make and remake our world, and our world is outsideless. No other beings build a complete world around themselves in the way we do, so there is nothing else with which we can compare our world, and therefore no basis upon which we could describe our world either as being mere appearance compared with *this*, or as being more real than *that*. Our world is merely and uniquely just what it is, and just what we build: there is no other world, and therefore no basis for describing *our* world as being relatively real or unreal.

Try again: out there prior to language there is nothing but a continu-ously outpouring flux of jostling possibilities. Our language, as it fastens upon one group of the proffered possibilities, closes off or determines a bit of our world. So there is only Be-ing (the efflux of possible contingencies), and language, moving over it like the Spirit moving over the primal chaos in Genesis. And our language, moving continuously, highlighting this and then that, constantly makes and remakes both our world and ourselves.

Our world is outsideless. Beyond the alleged 'veil of sense' there is not any real world of physical objects, nor is there the void, either. The so-called veil of sense, which is already language-formed and therefore made intelligible as soon as we clap eyes on it, is not a veil at all. It doesn't veil anything. It has no 'beyond'. It is outsideless.

Look again at your present visual field. There aren't any things on the far side of the screen of sense-experience, nor is there nothing, the void, either. The screen of visual experience is outsideless. It has no beyond, just as it has no edge. Similarly, there is no real subject on the *near* side of the screen, either. The motion of our languge continually builds our changing world, and similarly builds our changing selves. That is all, all there is.

When we have fully grasped this new world-picture, we understand that there is no longer any basis for describing some world or realm as being either truly real or merely apparent. Things are merely what they are, and that is it.

> We have abolished the real world: what world is left? the apparent world perhaps? . . . But no! *with the real world we have also abolished the apparent world.*[4]

Our world is a plenum: it is as complete and full as language. It is also outsideless. There is nowhere for any alternative reality—perhaps superior, or perhaps merely other —to get a foothold. Therefore all talk of our world as being either solidly real, or as being but a dream, is out of place. Outsidelessly and with no alternative, our world is just what it is, and that's all. We need to learn to content ourselves with just what contingently *is*.

A number of corollaries need to be pointed out, even though they are very familiar after having been pointed out over and over again in the thought of the 1980s. The first is that the point of view I describe undermines a number of treasured distinctions: for the doctrine that *we* are the makers of truth undermines the distinction between truth and fiction; second, the doctrine that it is only by being formed by our language that our world becomes fully determinate undermines the distinction between fact and interpretation; and third, the doctrine that *we* shape everything undermines the distinction between nature and culture.

That much is clear enough, as is the general point that we are trying to give up the practice of invoking a supposedly preexistent order of ready-made objective truth in order to settle disputes. Contrary to what they say about us, we do continue to believe in reason; but our notion of reason is (once again) 'democratic'—that is, it requires continuous conversation and renegotiation. Democracy is neither natural nor easy. On the contrary, it is hard work: one must labour ceaselessly to maintain a decently stable consensus.

As for the consensus we currently have—the state of the argument, things as we now see them—we try to get into the habit of doing without 'reality'. We give up the idea that some objective and independent touchstone of reality can be found. There isn't any: we are on our own. There is no referee. We don't actually need one. We must and we can content ourselves with the world we have. I call this 'subtle positivism': it was Wittgenstein's position, and it helps us to state crisply the difference between nihilism and non-realism.

A nihilist is a person who says that 'There is Nothing out there. On the far side of the screen of experience, the void begins'. Phenomenalism, for example, is nihilistic. Non-realism, however, sets out to prevent the spectres of the void and nothingness from being conjured up at all. Non-realism says: 'The screen of sense-experience is what it is: it *has* no beyond. There *is* no far side. Similarly, within your subjectivity, in your 'mind', nothing underlies the jumble of scurrying words and feelings that you are pleased to call "thought". It is just what it is.'

So my answer to the question of 'ultimate reality' is that we should give up the idea. The search for it is a quixotic, illusory quest. We should give up the idea of degrees of reality, and still more should we give up the idea that whatever has the highest degree of reality is of the greatest religious importance to us.

This discussion gives us the opportunity for a brief treatment of the question of dreaming and objective reality, which some may think deserves a place among the big questions:

How can I know for sure whether I am awake or dreaming?
Are we all dreaming?
Are we all perhaps characters in someone *else*'s dream—maybe God's?

This question has a long history in philosophy and popular philosophy, from the evil demon of René Descartes to the recent *Matrix* films. In the 1970s and 1980s there was a long debate about the answer to the question: 'How do we all know that we are not brains in a vat, being fed all our experiences by a great computer?' This debate presumably prompted *The Matrix*.

The question asks, 'Have we an independent and reliable criterion of objective reality?' and I have already given my answer, which is that when we decided to base truth and reality just on our own human consensus, we effectively gave up all ideas of looking for 'absolute' foundations for thought and knowledge. It is a mistake to give up foundationalism and then, a few moments later, to go back to it.

So I think *The Matrix* is hokum. We cannot be as comprehensively deluded as *that*, because objectivity can never be as 'absolutely' guaranteed as the film presupposes it might be. To demand absolutes, either way, is to make the same sort of mistake as is made by the person who won't eat any GM foods until he has 'absolute proof' that they are all safe. However the whole question of whether we have or can hope to establish a reliable independent criterion of objective reality is philosophically quite difficult, and I don't think that 'Am I awake or dreaming?' can quite be reckoned one of the great questions for the purposes of this book. When ordinary people in ordinary language ask: 'Am I awake or dreaming?' we should probably understand them to be saying something like: 'I can't believe my eyes. What's going on here?'—and no more than that.

9

THE GREAT QUESTION OF MY LIFE

Everyone knows what the expression, 'the love of his life' means, and I think everyone also knows what the expression 'his life's work' means. Human lives are often very untidy. People may begin and then subsequently abandon a variety of projects and relationships. But as the years go by it is often easy to recognize that one particular love-relationship or one particular body of work matters more to a person than any other. This is where his heart is, it is this to which she will in the end always come back, this is the relationship or the work in and through which she is best *identified*.

As a life may be unified around one great love-relationship or one great work, so according to Heidegger every major thinker has a dominant, unifying thought, to which he—or she, perhaps—keeps on returning. This 'one thought' may be compared, perhaps, with a painter's 'signature' works. These are the works that in their style are most unmistakably that artist's, the works that everyone recognizes immediately. Every big art gallery would like to have one of that particular artist's signature works in its holding.

I suggest that as a person's life may revolve around and may be identified through one great love, or one work, or a characteristic style, so a person typically has his own preoccupations, his own obsessions, his own angle upon the great questions of life. And so much is this true that in such a case I believe we'd be justified in saying that, 'The great question of his life has always been such and such'. I mean that he has worried away about this particular issue all his life. It is almost as if the great questions of life are not really questions at all, because they are never going to get answered

69

to the general satisfaction: rather, they remain lifelong issues and worries, and they strike different people in different ways. To know in a particular case what they are is to have gone a long way towards understanding that particular person's life.

A few simple examples: Death is obviously a universal fact of life, something that everyone needs to think about and form a view of; but it is not the same in everyone. On the contrary, the question about death figures very differently in different people's lives, and affects them very differently. For René Magritte, the key event is the drowning of his mother when he was a child. The image of a drowned, masked or shrouded, mysterious female body haunts his work, and affects his whole sense of the mystery of life. For Alfred Tennyson the key events are the rapidly developing historicized science of geology, bringing with it the new and shocking ideas of vast aeons of prehuman pasttime and great numbers of extinct animal species—and, against this background, the death of his beloved Arthur Henry Hallam. Tennyson struggles with the dreadful thought that someone very near and dear to him is now as extinct as a fossil. And third, for Philip Larkin what matters most is the intense horror he feels at the thought of his own steadily approaching extinction. Nowhere, I think, does he mourn someone else: he thinks only of his own dread at what is coming to him.

Three men: Magritte, Tennyson, and Larkin. All three of them were very troubled about the question of death and personal immortality. But they were not just three different individuals confronted by one and the same universal fact. On the contrary, each of the three appropriated the question of death and made it his own in his unique way. You could say that for each of them the death of the individual was the great question of his life—but they made three very different questions out of it.

I have over the years talked with many people as they approached death, and I have gained the strong impression that not only is nearly everyone aware of the great questions of life, but also everyone has a personal angle upon them. One man very close to me was haunted by the thought of insignificance and oblivion, and he wanted to be remembered. In his last years he bought some pieces of high quality antique furniture, and made specific dispositions of them in his will, by way of giving his heirs cause to remember him. He was not especially concerned about personal immortality, but he wanted not to be utterly forgotten. Another, a cousin who has just died, was concerned about his place in the world and became one of those who nowadays uses the Internet to help him draw up an elaborate genealogy of his family. Perhaps he thought: 'By understanding my genealogy I can get a little nearer to understanding who I am, and where I belong'. A woman relative was like many other women, I guess, in that she had only one great wish as she approached death: to meet her dear ones again. But can one, dare one, believe such a thing anymore? Another woman, a nonagenarian, had spent most of her life as an agnostic fellow-traveller of Christianity. People often call themselves agnostics by way of deferring the great questions, keeping them at arm's length until 'later on' (i.e., in old age) when, as we like to suppose, they will surely have become much easier to deal with. So now she had definitely reached old age, and being bedridden had plenty of time to address those troublesome long-deferred questions. But (of course) she felt completely flummoxed by them, and urgently demanded help and support. Rather late in the day, I fear. Young people are apt to think that with advancing age, when we have had our lives, we will find death closer, easier to live with, and easier to understand and accept. Not true.

I am suggesting that most people are aware of the great questions, and most people work out their own way of handling them (or deferring them, as the case may be). Most people appropriate the questions or obsess about them in their own characteristic way. In the case of most people it is appropriate to ask what has been the great question of his or her life. And the answer to that question shows what that individual's personal philosophy of life has been. More than that, it is probably the best clue we will ever have to who a person really is. For many people, and especially I think young ones, the first and chief of the great questions is:

Who am I? 11

The best way to answer this question is to retort with another: What has turned out to be your distinctive 'take' on the great questions of life? What are your obsessive preoccupations: around what philosophical questions and anxieties has your life revolved? *That* is who you are: I mean that your distinctive personal take on the great questions is the best indicator of who you really are. It reveals the rub, the pressure point, the point where the shoe pinches, what really gets to you. In which case we may be led to regard the great questions as being not just questions, but *tests* of character and perhaps cruces for our personal development.

Thus I am suggesting that living with the great questions, revolving them in one's mind and gradually forming a view of them, is nowadays an important part of religion because it is an important part of one's journey to selfhood. Until about 1830 or so most ordinary people in the West regarded themselves as living a world that was religiously pretty stable. At least, it was not necessary to be forever inspecting and digging up the foundations. Today everyone is aware of vast changes in worldview, in morality, and increasingly in religion. Everyone adopts a pilgrim view of life, and everyone is aware of having a personal religious history of changes imposed upon them by the changing times. They look back and find themselves forced to recognize that—without their having any clear understanding of how it has happened—the mere passage of the years has fundamentally changed their values and their core beliefs.

Against this background I have very much wanted to persuade people to take an interest in pure speculative philosophical and religious thinking—because that of course is what we all need. But how are ordinary people to be so persuaded? I have suggested that the correct procedure is one that is almost entirely new in the history of philosophy and theology: we should begin to take the thought of ordinary people seriously. In the *Everyday Speech* books of 1999–2000 I proposed that we could do this by collecting and studying interesting new idioms as they arrive in ordinary language, and I hope that the two life-books have proved that point.[1]

Here I am taking a further step. I am suggesting that we should also take seriously ordinary people's thinking about what are variously called *the ultimate questions, the big questions,* and *the great questions of life.* This is an exceedingly novel and heretical thing to propose; but then, my philosophical heresies are just as vile as my religious ones. Wittgenstein, like so many philosophers, was intensely irritated by the intellectual sloppiness and self-indulgence of the language in which the great questions of life are commonly formulated. He was annoyed by the popular assumption that goofy talk about 'the meaning of life' is philosophy. And I see what he means: in the past I have often made unkind remarks about popular ideas of 'philosophy' myself. But, nevertheless, I have now changed my mind. We may dislike the woolliness of the talk (*'What's the point of it all?' 'What does anything matter?'*) but, for good or ill, this is the language in which ordinary people are trying to sort out their basic philosophies of life. We should listen carefully to what they are saying, and we will find that a lot of it will turn out to be more interesting than we expected. The fact is that in the religious and philosophical crisis of our times people are ruminating constantly about the great questions of life, and are aware of being pilgrims who are making a great intellectual journey. We ought to listen to them, join them, and do what we can to help the conversation to become more articulate.

There was a period in the history of the novel—Cervantes to Smollett, perhaps?—when each new character who turned up in a novel would promptly spend twenty pages recounting his life history. It's like that today: because we live in a time of acute religious crisis and transition, everybody has a personal story of religious change and growth to tell and is grateful to be given any opportunity to tell it. Such testimonies perhaps used to be tales of sin, repentance, and conversion of life; but not anymore. Now they are stories that in a broad sense revolve around the great questions and our changing attitudes to them. For example, a typical story might relate how I used to get my sense of who I am, my place in the scheme of things, and the destined course of my life from orthodox religious belief; but I gradually lost all that and have instead come to see that one can live, one can find happiness in many small things in life, and one can do good 'in minute particulars', without the old confident sense of cosmic backing. George Eliot was perhaps one of the first to tell such a personal story, through the character of Dorothea and in the Preface to *Middlemarch*.[2]

You may well expect me to report on the great questions in my own life. I knew from the age of about fourteen or fifteen that I was of a speculative disposition, and the questions I asked were commonplace enough. What am I? What is this world about me? How do we come to be here? If nothing is necessary, and everything just *happens* to be as it is, how is it that everything presents itself as being so warm, coherent, and beautiful? At fifteen I was intensely attracted by Darwinism and took up biology just as many young people today are taking up psychology, i.e., as the subject that we hope will best help us to understand who and what we are. But I gradually came to understand that the scientific sort of understanding is as from the point of view of a disengaged ideal observer. It leaves out *oneself*, and therefore could never give me quite the all-round, ethically engaged, self-involving kind of understanding that I sought.

This realization drove me first to religion (whose charms and whose self-involving character are more obvious), and then to philosophy. I was always bothered by universal contingency. If everything just *happens* to be, and if every connection in the world only *happens* to hold, why doesn't everything accelerate out of control and crash, or alternatively just fall apart? I felt acute 'ontological insecurity', unable to see how the world holds together and manages to be as stable as it is.

To escape from this problem, I took up the old religious and philosophical remedies. One needed to find some first principle of things, or foundation, or starting point. One needed, perhaps, to find some self-evident truth, necessary and indubitable: something necessarily existing or self-guaranteeing: some infinite monarch. So around the ages of seventeen to twenty years I became involved with Plato and Descartes in philosophy, and with first Evangelicalism and then Anglo-Catholicism in religion.

At this stage I was still within the ambit of the traditional great questions. I was looking outside life in the hope of finding some infinite first principle or monarch that would support life, stabilize it, and give to it its law. In short, I was still thinking in terms of traditional metaphysical theism. I wanted, and I believed that there was, an objective God. But by twenty-one I had met Spinoza, Hume, Kant, and Wittgenstein, and was beginning to change. In the long term this meant that I would completely give up the idea that the meaning of life is to be found somewhere outside life, and instead would try to take up and carry through systematically the idea of *the outsidelessness of life*.

In philosophy this meant moving from the traditional British metaphysics (i.e., Plato, Aristotle, Descartes) to a consistently post-metaphysical outlook. In religion it meant giving up the traditional amphibian (or two-worlds) type of Christianity which always has half an eye on another and higher world, in favour of a new religion of total commitment just to this life, in all its contingency and uncertainty.

Thus we see that my own development seems to illustrate the rule I proposed earlier. Fuzzy, irritating, and badly worded though they may often seem, the popular great questions are important to us. In many ways a person's spiritual biography remains the story of how she personally appropriates the great questions, and how her lifelong reflection on them gradually changes her and shows her 'who she really is'.

10

In many different spheres of life, when we are challenged to explain and justify some thing, or belief, or practice, we do so by tracing it back to an original founding person or principle. Given our interest in genealogy and our veneration for our forebears, it is not at all surprising that almost everywhere people maintain that such and such a custom is followed, or such and such a rule is the law, because it was so ordained by the tribal ancestor who was our first Father and lawgiver in the beginning. In Bronze Age and later thought this search for a normative origin often becomes the search for an *arche*—a foundation, first principle, beginning, or element. The genealogical enquiry that traced everything back to a tribal ances-tor has thus been demythologized into a chain of causes, or motions, or relations of dependency that reaches back to a first cause, a prime mover, or a necessary being. The origin is always one, golden, lucid, and unmis-takeably authoritative, but over the years the state of primitive perfection that it first established has gradually decayed. We've passed through Silver, Bronze, and Iron Ages until now the times are 'partly of iron, partly of clay'.[1] History is always a process of slow decline, and to renew itself it must return again into its golden origin.

Thus it is that when we seek clearer understanding, when we seek jus-tifications, and when we seek reform and renewal, we retain even to this day a strong impulse to go outside present reality and try to return into a primitive golden unity and certainty. People still tend to think that scien-tific stories about how the universe, or life, or the human race *began* will help us to understand what the universe, or life, or human existence *really is*, that the original meaning of a word is still its *real* meaning, and that we can perhaps get closer to the meaning of great works of art if we can replicate the conditions—the musical instruments, the theatre—of their first performance. Even in philosophy many people are still persuaded by the old argument that to avoid scepticism, to avoid an indefinite regress, and to avoid circularity, every argument has to begin from at least one premiss that is accepted dogmatically because it is self-evidently true and indubitable. The rule is that, to get going, one needs to start from a founding certainty. Things are most themselves, and meanings are clearest, at their *beginnings*.

Because it is so ancient, religious thought of course remains steeped in these ancient foundationalist assumptions, with all their corollaries about everything having been better in the old days, about the wisdom of sticking close to what tradition prescribes, and so on. As we have seen in looking at the great questions of life, even to this day most people seem to assume that the purpose of life, the real meaning of life, the point of it all, the goal of life, what life is all about must be something great that is hidden outside life. I thought the same myself, at first. Only very gradually, through the influence of figures like Hume and Darwin, did I gradually come to admit the superior beauty and clarity of naturalistic or immanent types of explanation in all fields.

The general rule is that everything is contingent; everything is the product of time and chance. The cases of living organisms, of language, and of culture generally all persuade us that complex, ordered, rule-governed, and self-maintaining or self-replicating systems can be formed and can develop just by the interplay of contingent forces within the world, over long periods of time. And this implies that we do not need to be dominated by the models of a chain that is no stronger than its weakest link, or a building that is erected on secure foundations. There are other forms that a strong system of knowledge can take. In particular, a broad, spreading network of purely contingent truths can be immensely strong without having to be based upon any sort of external support or founding certainties.

To mark and to insist upon the victory of naturalistic explanation we eventually introduce, and argue vehemently for, the idea that the world—and that means above all the world of human life, the world we call just 'life'—is outsideless. We don't need any absolutes, or any external support: a world in which everything is relative can hang together surprisingly well, just as liberal democracy, although often believed to be "soft", turns out in fact to be a much stronger form of society than absolute monarchy.

The idea that life is outsideless may be compared with the idea in modern physical cosmology that the universe is finite but unbounded. Ordinary language still contains a few idiomatic phrases that refer to 'the four corners of the earth' or 'the ends of the earth'. Such phrases must date from a period when the world was not yet fully explored and mapped. We could then imagine that in some remote spot one might discover that one had come to the end of the world, and there was no farther that one could go. But today, when we are quite clear that Earth is a sphere and that the surface of a sphere is a finite area without any boundaries, we can easily see that Earth doesn't literally have any corners or ends or edges at all. On the contrary, if you set off in a straight line around the world in any direction, you will after only about 25,000 miles find yourself back at your starting point. Look about you, anywhere: on the globe's unbounded surface we are always in the middle and never on the rim.

Modern physical cosmology simply presents us with a three-dimensional version of the same idea. Three-dimensional space is, as it were, curved in such a way that again, if you set off in a straight line you will eventually return to your starting point. It is finite but unbounded: you never come to an edge, and it has no outside. This idea elegantly disposes of certain paradoxes that seem to arise for the Newtonian universe, whether it be supposed to be infinite or finite. For if a Newtonian universe be supposed finite, what happens at the edge of space? But if it be supposed infinite, then surely every straight line running away from you in any direction must eventually encounter a star, from which light and gravitational pull will come back at you. Won't that have the effect of flooding the universe with far too much light and gravitational force? So the new cosmology that pictures the universe as finite but unbounded is in certain ways simpler and clearer than the Newtonian picture; and this analogy shows how one may claim that the human lifeworld is finite but unbounded. You shouldn't think of needing to go outside it to explain its endless variety, and you shouldn't even try. Life is such that we are always in the midst of it, and never on the rim—a consideration that makes any idea of a supernatural order redundant.

More than that: as Meister Eckhart and others point out, it belongs to the very idea of life that it is spontaneously upwelling and self-affirming, just in the present tense. It is not secondary and must not be subordinated or devalued. Joyously, without needing anybody's permission or authority, life just springs up and renews itself. Life is its own ground, gratuitously. And when I say that life is outsideless, I do so by way of putting down a marker: we give notice of our intention firmly to oppose all those past and now obsolete ways of thinking that encouraged us to look for the point or purpose or meaning of life *outside* life. Life is a primary good and is always presupposed: we are always in life, and have to be so in order to gain access to any other goods. We plan to resist the ulteriority of a kind of thinking that always seeks to subvert the primacy of life. So on this point of the outsidelessness and the primacy of life I am at one with Nietzsche.

Finite but unbounded, all-inclusive, baggy and shapeless, including all the opposites of happiness and misery, good and ill-fortune, and including all the faiths, all the philosophies, and all the political ideologies, life is everything. It just goes on endlessly in all directions. Like marriage but even more so, it has to be accepted as a package deal. You can't pick and choose. What life is, is best reflected in our modern totalizing art forms—the novel, the feature film, the soap opera, the Sunday newspaper. And there is no way out of it: Dante imagined that somewhere there was a cave down which one could go to the underworld, and somewhere in the Antipodes a very high mountain up which one could climb into purgatory and heaven. But for us there is no way out of life and into somewhere else. When other people die, we see that they have ceased to play any part in life. They have slipped into the past tense. Only their 'remains' are still with us—the corpse, personal effects, memories. But they have not 'passed away' to another place. Life has no outside, and all ideas of a secret doorway into another world are fantasies. There are no secret doorways: life is a continuum.

That's life. And I'm saying all this to persuade you that there is nothing else for us except commitment to the living of life now, in the present tense. The young Heidegger assigned this alarm-bell role to the thought that we are mortal and have only a limited time left. I'm saying, though, that what best awakens us and brings us back to life is the realization that life is outsideless, and that it is futile to suppose that the value, the meaning, the point, the purpose of life could be located in some other realm outside life.

This brings me into sharp disagreement with the world-renouncing strain that quickly crept into early Christianity:

> Do not love the world or the things in the world. If anyone loves the
> world, love for the Father is not in him. For all that is in the world, the
> lust of the flesh and the lust of the eyes and the pride of life, is not of the
> Father, but is of the world. And the world passes away, and the lust of it;
> but he who does the will of God abides for ever.[2]

This passage is intellectually muddled in its association of 'the Father' with a realm somehow outside and *opposed* to 'the world' or to life. But, even worse, it is disastrously wrong in supposing that a human being should turn away from and renounce 'the lust of the flesh and the lust of the eyes and the pride of life'. We should be highly suspicious of language like that. It smacks of rationalist-ascetical hatred of life, and desire to mortify natural feeling. In flat opposition to asceticism, we should insist that there can be no lasting and secure human happiness or well-being except on the basis of good emotional health. In the past, religions and political ideologies have often been inspired by disgust at life's excessiveness, unsystematizability, and gratuitous self-affirmation. Life's burgeoning seems to such people almost obscene. They have sought to get life under control, by confining it within a disciplinary rational system. But such disciplinary systems create acute personal unhappiness, and of course life always fights back by seeking some way of overflowing and breaking out of them—a fact that we should welcome.

I conclude that when we speak of life as outsideless and as springing up gratuitously, we are rejecting traditional asceticism, rationalism, and all the systems of thought and of social discipline that try to plan life and get it under strict control. We choose freedom rather than order, and a touch of romantic excess rather than resigned acceptance of limitation. That is how we are able to pursue our salvation within the lifeworld, by going along with and trusting life's restless, excessive energy. The alternative route, which tries to master life and transcend it on the way to salvation in another world beyond life, is no longer open to us.

The older ecclesiastical sort of religion tried to bring life under the control of reason. It was disciplinarian, long-termist, and (I am sorry to say) deeply unhappy. Instead, in the new purely immanent and outsideless world of life, we should rather put our trust in life's endless battle to escape rational control and affirm itself in ever-new ways.

11

'IS THERE ANYBODY OUT THERE?'

You may think that the next great question belongs with question 7, because it surely belongs with that little group of old puzzles which used to be the subject of myths, but today have been taken over by science. Not quite, I think. It does seem clear that science has already completely taken over, or will very soon finish persuading us of its ability completely to take over, the questions about the origins of the universe, life on earth, the human race, and consciousness. So that is all satisfactory. But the next question is a little more problematic:

> *Are we alone?*
> *Is there anybody out there?*
> *'The truth is out there'. (Currently popular saying)*

12

Human beings have a strong propensity to imagine parallel worlds, and to suppose that the unknown will turn out to be more or less a repeat of the known. Thus folklore delights in imagining beings rather like ourselves, organized in societies rather like ours, in parallel worlds at the bottom of the sea (mermen), mining in the deepest caves under the greatest mountains (dwarves), or attending Queen Mab in a hidden kingdom in the depths of the forest or 'under the hill' (fairies). Similar speculations about quasi-human societies living on the moon and the planets go back almost as far as Giordano Bruno (1548–1600), and for obvious reasons. The ideas of Nicholas Copernicus removed Earth from its former unique position at the centre of the universe and made it instead just one of a number of planets circling the sun. What were those other planets like? The likeliest presumption seemed to be that they were rather like Earth—and perhaps they also resembled Earth in being inhabited. For that matter, perhaps most stars, perhaps indeed every star, had a system of planets orbiting it. In which case the same arguments from analogy may very well apply again, and the universe may turn out to be teeming with life on countless planets circling countless suns.[1]

So it was argued by a number of writers of the seventeenth to nineteenth centuries, writers who obligingly supplied the public with a stream of fictional accounts of journeys to the moon, to Mars, and so on. But as everyone knows, during the twentieth century rapid technical advance enabled us to take a much closer look at our neighbours, and our enthusiasm for life on other planets cooled considerably. Most of the universe seems to be a bleak desert, and the distances between stars with planetary systems look too great ever to be traversable within a single lifetime.

It is against this background of disappointment that question 12, *Are we alone?* has emerged as the most vivid example of a *new* great question—one that has arisen only in modern times. Belief in God has faded, the universe seems almost unimaginably vast and alien, and human beings feel more than ever a great need for confirmation. We seek some kind of independent validation of our general worldview, our scientific knowledge, our beliefs, our values, and above all, our sense that human life is interesting and important. Question 12, *Are we alone?* is a cry in the dark. Inevitably, we treat it as a scientific question. Inspired by the discovery of pulsars in the 1960s, enthusiasts with access to radio telescopes listen out for any kind of patterned radio emission from the stars, rather as three or four centuries ago little bands of enthusiasts were still occasionally seen on hilltops scanning the night sky hopefully for signs of the Second Coming of Christ.

In a word, question 12, *Are we alone?* presents itself as a factual question that may one day be settled by a sudden great scientific discovery. But really the motivation is and remains quasi-religious. The yearning for objective confirmation that drives it is never likely to be satisfied, I fear—by which I mean that the satisfying discovery that people are aching for is never at all likely to be made. What gives us away and makes our longings implausible is our determination to believe that, when we contact them, they will turn out to be very like us. I can tell you: they will not. I concede that it is just possible that we will one day discover extraterrestrial life and even evidence of extraterrestrial intelligence. But we have little reason for thinking that extraterrestrial life will resemble terrestrial life, and even less for expecting that they will speak a language that is translatable into our language. For supposing that they will be anything like company for us we have no reason at all. Nevertheless, the desire to believe that we are not alone will no doubt continue, for it is a *religiously* insatiable thirst. It is closely related to epistemological *realism*, the perennial desire of so many scientists to believe that their current theory—although it is only of very recent origin, and will in due course become obsolete—is objectively true. *The truth is out there*, goes the popular slogan. It sounds like a rational statement of confidence in the objectivity of one's own knowledge. It sounds like a robust statement of Enlightenment faith in objective reason. But in reality it is a cry in the dark—a futile cry.

Hence I have to confess that I feel less sympathy for the question '*Are we alone?*' than for any of the other great questions. We live over a century after the death of Nietzsche, whose works are nowadays on every undergraduate's bookshelf. We ought to have grasped by now the implications of the obvious post-Darwinian fact that we ourselves invented all the words in our language—our whole vocabulary, including all our leading concepts. *We* invented truth, *we* invented objectivity, *we* invented reality. Ideas such as these were not lying about on the ground, waiting for us to pick them up. Nobody sent them to us through the post. We invented them, and their meaning and their value to us is given by the part they actually play in our exchanges.

I'm saying that we ought to have grasped by now that our language is our world. It is a continuum, and we made it all. The idea that it needs—or could be given—any confirmation *from outside* is a complete mistake. You wouldn't walk up to a group of Welsh speakers, listen to them for a bit, and then pat them on the back and assure them that they are communicating successfully, would you? They don't need to be told by you; and by the same token the human race in general doesn't need to be told that the common world we've all built and the common laws and values we've managed to establish are all right. We don't need to be told. A working language and a working world are just what they are, and fine as they are. Confirmation is not needed. Indeed, the very idea of it is highly dubious. What sort of beings would be in a position to give it? Are we humans in a position to pat whales on the back and tell them that the various sounds they make are doing a great job?

So I am suggesting, through the doctrines of outsidelessness and radical humanism, that we should give up all ideas of external validation or endorsement. They aren't needed, and we will never get it.

12

The next great question expresses a dubious, dawning sense of cosmic disappointment. It arises in a situation where we have been led to expect great things of some thing or occasion. It's going to be really important to us: it will change our lives. So the expected moment arrives—but it's an anticlimax. It's a bit of a letdown. Our expectations are disappointed. When we say 'Is that *it*?' we are asking if what has just been presented to us can *really* be the thing of which we had been entertaining such high hopes.

This sense of cosmic letdown is expressed in a few brief but pregnant English phrases:

Is that it?
Is that all?
Was that it?

One has heard this doubt and disappointment voiced sometimes in connection with Confirmation and First Communion, or marriage and first sex. The only cases where the reality regularly turns out to exceed people's expectations are great works of art—especially paintings, and sometimes sculpture and architecture. The discovery that the real thing is even better than one had always imagined it to be strikes people as being so rare, joyous, and overwhelming that they often feel faint, or indeed do faint outright. Others report that tears come to their eyes.

85

A few examples from personal experience are here cited simply for pleasure: the sculpture at Reims, as well as the great battered building; Michelangelo's horned Moses in Rome; the Botticellis in the Uffizi Gallery; the interiors of King's College Chapel and Sherborne Abbey; Durham Cathedral seen from the college across the river valley *floating* above a dense white cloud of early morning mist. Things like these will never disappoint, but otherwise the actual thing very rarely lives up to its advance billing. *Is that it?* we say, somehow managing to lay a scornful emphasis both upon the second word and upon the third. And one might say the same about life itself, which began with such high hopes but then in every case turns out to be a long process of gradual disillusionment and increasing constriction.

Poets contrast the boundlessness of our aspirations with the severely limited character of anything that we can actually achieve:

> This is the monstrosity in love, lady, that the will is infinite, and the execution confined; that the desire is boundless, and the act a slave to limit.[1]

Some have made of this disproportion an argument for immortality. If Earth cannot satisfy, then heaven will:

> Ah! but a man's reach should exceed his grasp
> Or what's a heaven for?[2]

But that is a clear mistake, and a relic of pre-Darwinian thinking. From the obvious biological fact that life is insatiably restless and always craves more, it does not in the least follow that we must have been created to live forever. Rather, the point is that creatures like the indolent and undersexed giant panda, in which the life-impulse is not insatiably restless, just don't survive for long and (frankly) don't deserve to survive. Life has to be restless and insatiable to be itself. That is the secret that capitalism has understood. Temporal creatures like us need that endless, irritable dissatisfaction and driving restlessness to be anything, and to achieve anything at all. A contented, stable life in a rut is a living death. It is contemptible. Life without vitality, life without discontent, life without some kind of struggle for greatness—or, at the very least, excellence—is worthless.

It is along some such lines that we have to respond to the sense of cosmic disappointment voiced in the question under consideration: 'Is that it?' The question asked why is it that—apart from a few cases of great art—the actual almost always falls short of the ideal, and life never quite delivers as much as the doctrine appeared to promise? Why is it that we human beings seem to long for eternal happiness, but will only ever know time, restlessness, and finitude?

The answer is that life is time and we are time. We can't even clearly *think* that the conditions of life could be radically different from what they are. And, things being *as* they are, the very best that we human beings can ever know is a long, hard struggle, relieved now and again by brief unexpected moments of apocalyptic joy when we glimpse the top, we see what it's all about, and it all makes sense.[3] For a moment, one enjoys eternal happiness while still living in time. That's the summit, life's top. Such moments make it all worthwhile: for their sake one is happy to have lived, and feels ready to leave without lodging any complaint. Given that we are what we are, timebound talking animals pretty much in love with language, that's the nearest to 'heaven' or a state of eternal beatitude that we can ever hope to get.[4]

13

Until very recently a question about human destiny would surely have been included in everyone's list of the great questions of life. It was a question not merely about individual life after death, but about a hoped-for future completion and consummation of all history, an idea that could take many different forms. It might involve a cyclical picture of cosmic time and a return of the Age of Gold; it might involve the coming of the kingdom of God on Earth and the millennial reign of Christ and his saints; it might involve a general enlightenment and liberation of all humankind; it might involve the withering away of the state and the establishment of a communist society, or it might involve simply a catastrophic judgement and destruction of Earth. The 'one, far-off divine event, / To which the whole creation moves' has been very variously conceived, but its collapse in all forms has happened only since about 1973, and many echoes of the ancient hope are still heard in our language:

> . . . till kingdom come (i.e., a very long time ahead)
> Where will it all end?
> Where are we going?
> What will become of us?
> What is the world coming to?

14

Most of these phrases imply a growing anxiety and doubt about the long-term future, so that perhaps scepticism about traditional grand narratives telling of future redemption has been slowly increasing over a lengthy period. I have mentioned the year 1973 because I recall that it was in the mid-seventies that I first noticed that the belief in progress and 'the perfectibility of man' had just died, and because 1973 is sometimes cited as the year when the standard of living of American blue-collar workers finally stopped rising. The year 1973 was the year when the tide turned. It was also, of course, the year when Western consumers were forcefully reminded of the finitude of the earth's natural resources, such as oil.

Today, the picture of a future glorious consummation of the whole world-historical process has finally faded from people's minds. The question of human destiny has ceased to be one of the great questions. It has been taken over by science, and our thinking about the long-term future is now entirely dominated by extrapolations of present trends, guesses about the future development of technology, and so on. Religion, philosophy, and political ideology appear to be making no contribution at all to thinking about the human prospect.

The upshot is that whereas question 6 survives as one of the great questions, question 14 has dropped off the list completely. While it lasted, the threat of nuclear annihilation had some power to revive traditional apocalyptic thinking, but even that has now faded. We face instead a dull prospect: in a few centuries we will very probably have made the earth uninhabitable, and we will die out. It might be possible to avert this fate if we could find and cultivate some motive or value strong enough to override the competitive nationalism and the concern for economic growth that rule us at present, but there seems little likelihood of that. The big coming nations, China, India, Russia, and Brazil, will simply race on unstoppably until global disaster overtakes us all.

Predictively, the future is death; and as a topic of serious religious thought, the future is dead. Accordingly I have for years moved religious thought and the concern for salvation into the present tense. In the short run eternal happiness is (briefly) attainable in the present moment, and in the long run we are all dead. Such is the present position: but it leaves me with a doubt. Is it possible, at this very late date, to talk about reviving a religious concern for the course and outcome of the human project as a whole? It has proved possible to persuade people to take a great deal of trouble and pay a substantial premium in order to rescue and preserve portions of the natural environment and some animal species. Might it be possible along similar lines to get people interested in a hugely costly effort to preserve the environment as a whole, and the human species?

* * * * *

Question (14)—in parentheses because it has become an ex-question—was about eschatology, the doctrine of the last things. It has fallen off the list: we seem to have tacitly abandoned all forms of the idea that individual lives, and world-history as a whole, are being guided towards a future consummation, a destiny already planned and prepared for them. Instead we extrapolate present trends and make predictions on the basis of present theory, using the results to steer our own behaviour towards desirable outcomes. So much for our future hope.

There is also a question (15)—in parentheses, again—which deserves mention in conclusion. It is about evil:

> *Unde malum / Whence is evil?*
> *Where has evil come from?*
> *Why do we suffer?*
>
> **15**

In Christian theology God is perfectly good, and cannot be the author of evil. The world as God created it must originally have been quite free from evil and suffering. They must be regarded as secondary intrusions into a world in which they originally had no place; so it seems reasonable to ask how they have arisen—and Christian theology then told its stories of the revolt of Lucifer, the rebellion in heaven and its defeat, the fall of man and so on.

While the opening chapters of Genesis were a major influence upon the common worldview, the question about the nature and origin of evil and suffering remained an obvious big question. But with the rise of our modern historical sciences of nature, and the consequent shift to a much more life-centred worldview, evil, suffering, conflict, and death have been naturalized. They are all part of life, part of the struggle for existence, part of the whole package. We can scarcely imagine life without contingency (risk), hardship, competition, struggle for survival, and so on. If we observe other living things closely we cannot fail to be impressed by their extraordinarily intense relish for life, and their matter-of-fact acceptance of the dark side of life when it finally hits them—as it always does. And doesn't that suggest a moral for us?

Evil and suffering are of course just as great as they have always been. But we are beginning to see them as part of life's package deal. They don't present quite so deep an intellectual problem as they once seemed to. Question (15) has accordingly dropped off the list.

Appendix

A. Questions about the meaning, point, purpose, or worth of It All

   1 *Why are we here?*
     Why were we put on this earth?
     What are we here for?

   2 *What is the meaning of life?*
     What is the point of it all?
     What's it all supposed to mean?
     What's it all about?

   3 *Does it matter?*
     What's the point?
     Does anything matter?
     What does it all matter?
     'In the long run we are all dead'. (J.M. Keynes)
     'If Darwin's right, we are just accidental by-products of a mean-
     ingless universe, and nothing we do makes any real difference'.
     (Popular evangelical apologetics)

B. Speculative questions in metaphysics and cosmology

   4 *Is there a God?*
     Does God exist?

   5 *Is death the end?*
     Are we, or do we have, souls?

6 *How did everything begin?*
How did life begin?
Who are we? Who made us?
How did consciousness begin? 'Can machines think?'

C. Questions about Be-ing, or finite being: questions, that is, about coming-to-be and passing-away; about temporality, contingency and finitude

7 *Why is it that anything at all exists: why is there not just nothing?*
It is not how things are in the world that is mystical, but that it exists. (Wittgenstein, TLP 6.44)

8 *Is the past real?*
Où sont les neiges d'antan? /*Where are the snows of yesteryear?*

9 *What does it all mean?*
It doesn't mean anything in particular, it just happens.
What am I meant to be doing / What am I cut out for?
If it has got your number on it, that's it.
That's it. (But see 13, below)

D. Supplementaries

10 *What is ultimately real?*
What is the nature of ultimate reality?

11 *Who am I?*
What is the great question of my life? / 'What has been my own personal take on the great questions of life?'

12 *Are we alone?*
Is there anybody out there?
'The truth is out there'.

13 *Is that it?*
Is that all?
Was that it?

(14 ... till kingdom come   ex-question
Where will it all end?
Where are we going?
What will become of us?
What is the world coming to?)

(15 Unde malum / Whence is evil?   ex-question
Where has evil come from?
Why do we suffer?)

(16 How can I know for sure whether I am awake
      or dreaming?   rejected
    Are we all dreaming?
    Is someone else—God, perhaps—dreaming us?

I have here attempted something that, I think, has not been done before:
I have tried to list and classify all the great questions of life, citing them in
the formulations that you are most likely to have heard people use. Please
write and tell me of any glaring omissions or errors that strike you.

In the case of the life-idioms and other idioms, I was quite quickly
and easily able to compare the situation in English with that in French,
German, and some other languages. In the case of the great questions, we
do not find such clearly fixed canonical wordings listed in dictionaries, so
that I cannot pretend to be able to draw up a list of the great questions
in any living language other than English. I believe I have a good ear for
English, and I know that I do not have an equally good ear for any other
language. However, I have been able to consult a number of friends who
are specialists in one or another European language, and their opinions
briefly confirm my own guess, which is that if we were to set out to list
them the great questions would come out much the same in all the major
European languages. But modern communications are getting to be so
good and cheap that the conversation of humanity is getting to be much
the same all around the world—which makes me inclined to say that the
great questions are probably very much the same for ordinary people
everywhere.

At the time of writing I have been unable to check the position as
regards the principal Asian languages.

Notes

Introduction

1 *An Empiricist's View of the Nature of Religious Belief.*

2 A realist view of religious beliefs sees them as describing supernatural facts and states of affairs: a non-realist view says that they are to be understood in terms of the rituals with which they are associated and the way of life that they inculcate.

Chapter 1 *Beginning all over Again*

1 Address: 'The Price of Free World Victory'. His book *The Century of the Common Man* was published the next year, in 1943.

2 'Live options'—a term introduced by William James—are choices that are momentous and unavoidable. Some choices are not urgent, because the issues involved are no longer 'alive'. They can be deferred. But a live option confronts us daily, and calls for a decision.

3 *The New Religion of Life in Everyday Speech; Life, Life.*

4 *Philosophy's Own Religion.*

5 *Reforming Christianity.*

6 *Emptiness and Brightness.*

7 *Emptiness and Brightness.*

8 Mark 2:27f.

Chapter 2 *The End of Dogmatic Thinking*

1 Gordon D. Kaufman of Harvard University has developed such a 'fictionalist' conception of systematic—or, as he calls it, 'constructive'—theology since the 1970s, and sets it out in *In Face of Mystery* (1993). His views closely resemble

those put forward by me during the same period, but are considered much more acceptable than mine.

2 This account of how we should interpret religious beliefs 'regulatively' rather than 'speculatively' comes from the tradition of Kant, Kierkegaard, and (especially) Wittgenstein, to whom I was much indebted during the 1980s.

Chapter 3 *Religion Without Beliefs*

1 I am referring here to the later Heidegger's reading of the history of philosophy.

2 The urgent demand for sudden, violent conversion and the speedy attainment of eternal religious happiness is a mixed blessing, because both in East Asian Buddhism and in Evangelical Protestant Christianity it leads to anti-intellectualism. When instant salvation is offered *Now*, there's nothing to be gained by thinking.

3 These are the moments that Nietzsche calls 'suprahistorical' (*Uber-geschichtlich*). For a short discussion and texts, see Robert M. Burns and Hugh Rayment-Pickard, *Philosophies of History*, part 5, pp. 131–54.

4 This belief that by cross-cultural studies of mysticism and religious experience one could develop a universal science of religion—or at least, *of human religiosity*—was widespread during the century after the pioneering work of William James. Its last peak in Britain is associated with the names of Sir Alistair Hardy, Edward Robinson, and David Hay at the Religious Experience Research Unit, Manchester College, Oxford. In recent years it has retreated, pushed back by the counter-assertion that all religious experience and writing is evidently culturally formed. The 'cognitive content' that we ascribe to our religious experiences is in every case put into them by us.

Chapter 4 *Approaching the Great Questions*

1 *Critique of Pure Reason*, p. 635.

2 Quoted in Bryan Magee, *The Philosophy of Schopenhauer*, p. 9.

3 See Friedrich Nietzsche, *Philosophy and Truth*, No. IV 'On the Truth and Lies in a Nonmoral Sense', pp. 79–97.

Chapter 5 *Getting the Horrors*

1 Near the beginning of the nineteenth century popular broadsheets were sold in England in two versions, 'penny plain' and 'tuppence coloured'.

2 For this and the previous paragraph, see my previous life-books, *The New Religion of Life in Everyday Speech* and *Life, Life*.

Chapter 6 *Religious Feeling, Healthy and Sick*

1 The literalism is shown in two linguistic points: Jesus speaks, not just of 'eating his body' but of 'chewing his flesh', with a suggestion of erotic 'eating up', or devouring.

Chapter 7 *Short Answers to the Great Questions*
1 *Tractatus*, 5.621, 6.431, 6.4311, etc.
2 *Ethics*, Part Four, Prop. LXVII.

Chapter 8 *The Question of 'Ultimate Reality'*
1 I Samuel 16:7. Our ultraconservative biblical scholars still want to date this book well before Plato! In fact, the use of the appearance/reality distinction here is only one of the many indications that the Hebrew Bible reached its final form at a very late date, and well after the rise of philosophy.
2 Anthony Kenny, *The Five Ways*.
3 This was the theme of David Lodge's novel, *Thinks . . .* (2001).
4 Friedrich Nietzsche, *Twilight of the Idols and The Anti-Christ*, p. 41.

Chapter 9 *The Great Question of My Life*
1 *The New Religion of Life in Everyday Speech*; *Life, Life.*
2 George Eliot, *Middlemarch* (1871–1872). An interestingly different, and typically modern, journey of self-discovery is also made by her *Daniel Deronda* (1876).

Chapter 10 *Outsidelessness*
1 Daniel 2:33.
2 I John 2:15–17.

Chapter 11 *'Is there anybody out there?'*
1 Arthur O. Lovejoy's pioneering work in the history of ideas, *The Great Chain of Being* (1936), has a good discussion of these matters.

Chapter 12 *Is that it?*
1 *Troilus and Cressida*, III, ii, 85.
2 Robert Browning, *Andrea del Sarto*, 1.97.
3 Luke 10:18, which is widely thought by scholars to preserve an original saying of Jesus, is one of the most vivid and memorable expressions of this type of 'apocalyptic joy' in the Bible. It reached Luke as an isolated saying, and to weave it into his narrative he had to find a suitable context for it. He did not succeed, and the saying sticks out very awkwardly from its implausible setting. Some commentators think it may reflect something said by Jesus in a state of trance. See R.W. Funk, Roy W. Hoover, and the Jesus Seminar, *The Five Gospels*, p. 321.
4 The *second* closest we can get is described in *The Way to Happiness*. It is 'cosmic emotion', an overflow of absorbed, unselfed aesthetic delight that I associate with great art and with certain landscapes, and see as being religiously valuable.

Bibliography

This is an impossible booklist to compile, because (as has been said) there is no precedent for a book that tries to gather together and make more explicit what people in general obscurely think and say about the great questions of life. It is true that there are a number of good books and anthologies that deal with 'the big questions' of metaphysics, but not all the big questions of metaphysics are big questions for ordinary people. Thus the great Nietzschean question. 'What is the point of truth and personal truthfulness even in cases where the truth is very bad news for us?'— that question, I say, which Bernard Williams' last book attempts to answer, is not really an ordinary person's question. The ordinary person is more concerned to know what we should go by, what we can rely on, in *life*, and therefore has an interest which is always intensely practical. However some Western philosophers—for example, Schopenhauer, Nietzsche, Heidegger, and Sartre—have shown a strong interest in the philosophy of life, and I have chosen a few titles that may help readers to track down this aspect of their thought. The earlier writers whom we most often hear quoted on these topics are of course Shakespeare and Pascal, and indeed the posthumous publication of Pascal's *Pensées* in 1670 has become perhaps the chief marker of the return of the great questions in the Modern period.

On the religious side, it happens that a few English writers have in one way and another argued for a closer study of the actual religious thought and behaviour of ordinary people, as distinct from the traditional polling about doctrinal beliefs by social psychologists, which merely asks how far ordinary people conform, or fail to conform, to official orthodoxy. These writers include Edward Bailey ('implicit religion'), Jeff Astley ('ordinary theology'), and Tim Jenkins ('everyday life'), and I have included an item by each of them.

I have also included a few popular introductions to philosophy. It is hard to cite equally good examples of good and popular but completely free and post-orthodox or post-dogmatic religious thought, unless one goes as far out as Krishnamurti and others like him. The book by Paul Heelas that is listed below does contain a large bibliography. Another way of seeking out genuinely free, nonecclesiastical religious thought is by studying the sort of cranky but highly talented 'lay' individual that the English tradition does so well: Blake, Hardy, D.H. Lawrence, Stanley Spencer, Damien Hirst. Try, for example, Kenneth Pople's biography of Spencer.

On the linguistic side there is nothing I can recommend, except perhaps the sketches of working-class culture illustrated with stock sayings and remembered from his childhood by Richard Hoggart in *The Uses of Literacy* (1957). I have to trust my own memory and feel for the language when, in the Appendix, I epitomize the ordinary person's view of the great questions in about fifty commonly heard sentences, and I am hoping that you will easily recognize virtually every sentence as one that you too have heard before. Checking with friends and family members suggests to me that among native English speakers there is well over 90 percent agreement about what is or is not established idiom.

Astley, Jeff.*Ordinary Theology: Looking, Listening and Learning in Theology.* Burlington, VT and Aldershot, England: Ashgate, 2002.

Bailey, Edward I. *Implicit Religion in Contemporary Society.* Kampen, Netherlands: Kok Pharos, 1997.

Batchelor, Stephen. *Buddhism Without Beliefs: A Contemporary Guide to Awakening.* New York: Riverhead Books, 1997.

Braithwaite, R. B. *An Empiricist's View of the Nature of Religious Belief.* Cambridge University Press 1955; last reprinted Bristol: the Thoemmes Press, 1994.

Britton, Karl. *Philosophy and the Meaning of Life.* Cambridge: the Cambridge University Press, 1969.

Burns, Robert M. and Hugh Rayment-Pickard. *Philosophers of History: From Enlightenment to Postmodernity.* Malden, MA, and Oxford: Basil Blackwell, 2000.

Cottingham, John. *On the Meaning of Life.* New York and London: Routledge, 2003.

Cupitt, Don. *Emptiness and Brightness.* Santa Rosa, CA: Polebridge Press, 2001.

———, *Kingdom Come in Everyday Speech.* London: SCM Press, 2000.

———, *Life, Life.* Santa Rosa, CA: Polebridge Press, 2003.

———, *The Meaning of It All in Everyday Speech*. London: SCM Press, 1999.

———, *The New Religion of Life in Everyday Speech*. London: SCM Press, 1999.

———, *Philosophy's Own Religion*. London: SCM Press, 2000.

———, *Reforming Christianity*. Santa Rosa, CA: Polebridge Press, 2001.

———, *The Way to Happiness*. Santa Rosa, CA: Polebridge Press, 2004.

Danto, Arthur C. *Sartre*. Fontana Modern Masters series. Glasgow: Fontana/Collins, 1975.

Funk, Robert W., Roy W. Hoover, and the Jesus Seminar, *The Five Gospels: The Search for the Authentic Words of Jesus*. New York: Scribner, 1993.

Gray, John. *Straw Dogs: Thoughts on Humans and Other Animals*. London: Granta Books, 2003.

Guignon, Charles B. ed. *The Cambridge Companion to Heidegger*. New York and Cambridge: Cambridge University Press, 1993.

Heelas, Paul. *The New Age Movement: The Celebration of the Self and the Sacralization of Modernity*. Oxford and Cambridge, MA: Basil Blackwell, 1996.

Heidegger, Martin. *The Question of Being*. Trans. William Kluback and Jean T. Wilde. London: Vision Press, 1959.

———, *Basic Writings*. Ed. David Farrell Krell. US edition, New York: Harper Collins, various dates; latest revised and expanded edition, London: Routledge, 1993.

Hoggart, Richard. *The Uses of Literacy*. London: Chatto and Windus, 1957.

James, William. *Essays in Radical Empiricism*. London and New York: Longmans, Green, 1912.

———, *The Will to Believe*. London and New York: Longmans, Green, 1896.

Jenkins, Timothy. *Religion in English Everyday Life*. New York and Oxford: Berghahn, 1999.

Kant, Immanuel. *The Critique of Pure Reason*. Trans. Norman Kemp Smith. London: Macmillan/New York: St Martin's Press, 1933 and many reprints, Book II, Transcendental Doctrine of Method, Chap. II, 'The Canon of Pure Reason', pp. 629–52.

Kaufman, Gordon D. *In Face of Mystery*. Cambridge, MA: Harvard University Press, 1993.

Kenny, Anthony. *The Five Ways*. London: Routledge and Kegan Paul, 1969.

Krell, David F. *Daimon Life: Heidegger and Life-Philosophy*. Bloomington and Indianapolis: Indiana University Press, 1992.

Larkin, Philip. *Collected Poems*. Ed. Anthony Thwaite. Boston and London: Marvell and Faber and Faber, 1988.

Lovejoy, Arthur O. *The Great Chain of Being; A Study of the History of an Idea*. Cambridge, MA: Harvard University Press, 1936.

Magee, Bryan. *The Philosophy of Schopenhauer*. Oxford: the Clarendon Press, 1983.

Mill, John Stuart. *Three Essays on Religion*, 1874.

Nagel, Thomas. *What Does It All Mean?* New York and Oxford: Oxford University Press, 1987.

Nietzsche, Friedrich. *Twilight of the Idols and The Anti-Christ*. Trans. R.J. Hollingdale. Harmondsworth and New York: Penguin Books, 1968.

——, *Philosophy and Truth: Selections from Nietzsche's Notebooks of the Early 1870s*. Ed. and trans. Daniel Breazeale. New Jersey: Humanities Press, 1979.

——, *The Will to Power*. Trans. Walter Kaufmann and R.J. Hollingdale, ed. Walter Kaufman. New York: Random House Vintage Books, 1968.

Pascal, Blaise. *Pensées*. Trans. A.J. Krailsheimer. Harmondsworth and Baltimore: Penguin Books, 1966.

Pattison, George. *The Later Heidegger*. New York and London: Routledge, 2000.

Rayment-Pickard, Hugh. *The Myths of Time: From Saint Augustine to American Beauty*. London: Darton, Longman and Todd, 2004.

Rhees, Rush, ed. *Ludwig Wittgenstein: Personal Recollections*. Oxford: Basil Blackwell, 1981, especially the contributions of C.M. Drury.

Rundle, Bede. *Why There Is Something Rather than Nothing*. Oxford and New York: Oxford University Press, 2004.

Russell, Bertrand. *The Problems of Philosophy*, 1912; modern editions, New York and Oxford: Oxford University Press, 1967, 1980, etc.

Ryan, Alan. *J.S. Mill*, London and Boston: Routledge, 1974, Chap. 8.

Sartre, Jean-Paul. *Being and Nothingness*. Trans. Hazel E. Barnes. London: Methuen, 1958 and many reprints.

——, *Existentialism and Humanism*. Trans. Philip Mairet. London: Methuen, 1948.

Schopenhauer, Arthur. *The World as Will and Representation*. Trans. E. F. T. Payne, 2 vols. New York: Dover, 1966.

Spinoza, Baruch. *Ethics*, Part Four, Prop. LXVII.

Tennyson, Alfred. 'In Memoriam A. H. H.' 1850.

Vaneigem, Raoul. *The Revolution of Everyday Life*. London: Practical Paradise Publications, 1975.

Wallace, Henry. *The Century of the Common Man.* New York, Reynal & Hitchcock, 1943.

Warburton, Nigel. *Philosophy: The Basics*. 3rd ed.. New York and London: Routledge, 1999.

Warnock, Mary. *The Philosophy of Sartre*. London: Hutchinson, 1985.

Williams, Bernard. *Truth and Truthfulness: An Essay in Genealogy*. Princeton NJ: Princeton University Press, 2002.

Wittgenstein, L. *Tractatus Logico-Philosophicus*. Trans. D. F. Pears and B. F. McGuinness. Oxford: Basil Blackwell, 1961.

Index